258
GREAT
DATES
WHILE YOU WAIT

258 GREAT DATES WHILE YOU WAIT

Susie Shellenberger & Greg Johnson

BROADMAN & HOLMAN PUBLISHERS

Nashville, Tennessee

© 1995
by Susie Shellenberger and Greg Johnson
All rights reserved
Printed in the United States of America

4261-77
0-8-54-6177-9

Dewey Decimal Classification: 306.73
Subject Heading: Dating (Social Customs)\ Youth—Religious Life
Library of Congress Card Catalog Number: 94-34346

Shauna Menefee's story first appeared in the April 1994 issue of *Brio* magazine, published
by Focus on the Family. "Dating Pointers from Point of Grace" by Susan Maffett first
appeared in the September 1994 issue of *Brio*.

"Sometimes Sex Sounds a Lot Like Love"
by Ruth Senter from *Campus Life* magazine, © 1994, published by Christianity Today, Inc.
Carol Stream, IL. Used by permission.

Library of Congress Cataloging-in-Publication Data

Shellenberger Susie.
    258 great dates while you wait / Susie
    Shellenberger, Greg Johnson.
        p.   cm.
    ISBN 0-8054-6177-9
    1. Dating (Social customs)—Case studies—Juvenile literature. 2. Dating (Social cus-
toms—Religious aspects—Christianity—Juvenile literature. 3. Sexual abstinence—Juvenile
literature.
[1. Dating (Social customs) 2. Christian life.] I. Johnson, Greg, 1956-   . II. Title. III.
Title: Fifty-eight great dates.
HQ801.s524   1995
646.7'7—dc20   94-34346
                                                                          CIP
                                                                           AC

To Michelle and Geoff Stevens. May all your dates be filled with good, old-fashioned fun. Thanks for including me in your family. You two are like a brother and sister to me. I believe in the exciting future God has in store for both of you!

Love,
Susie

To my sons, Troy and Drew. If this doesn't help with the opposite sex, nothing will!

Dad

SOME COOL STUFF IN THIS BOOK

WHY DO YOU  DATE?

Have you ever asked yourself why you want to date? If not, ask it now. (Go ahead, say it out loud. "Why do I want to date?")

There are many bad reasons to date: popularity, conquest, pressure from friends, nothing better to do. But then again, there are a few good reasons, too.

- You enjoy spending time with and getting to know the opposite sex.
- You know you can have some good, clean fun.
- You're attracted to him/her (God did that).
- You're wondering what type of person you want to live with for the rest of your life, so spending time with several becomes a good way to find out which personality best fits your own.

Some adults believe that allowing teenagers to date is like putting a kid in a candy shop. They think, *Teens are awakening to their sexuality and they're going to*

want to experiment. When they do, mistakes will be made and consequences will have to be faced—some deadly. It's better not to let them date at all during their high school years until they are mature enough to handle the pressure.

To a degree, this line of thinking is correct. A large percentage of teens—even Christian teens—aren't mature enough to handle the pressure. They forget that "True Love Waits." Unfortunately, many are swallowing the line Hollywood has fed them, that they can—and should—go from dating to sex, skipping the in-between steps of love and marriage.

But let's face reality. Unless you live in a home or go to a church that absolutely forbids contact between the sexes (which is probably doubtful since you're reading this book), you'll likely want to date. Whether dating begins in high school or college, it doesn't matter. It's perfectly normal to wait to date. In fact, did you know that less than 50 percent of high schoolers date *at all* before college?

So if you're ready to date . . . what will be YOUR goal in dating?

We believe the goal of dating should reflect the good guidelines above. If these are things you want to accomplish, this book is for you. We've filled these pages with tons of ideas to have fun, to get to know the other person, and to discover if you and someone else genuinely click together.

Every experience in life can teach you something. Have fun, but let the people you spend time with educate you about the opposite sex, about you, and about your relationship with God.

DATING DEFINED

It's never too early or too late to stop and think about what this whole dating thing is all about. You've already read about some good (and some not-so-good) reasons to date. But if dating is so important, how come it's a fairly *new* thing?

New? What in the world are you talking about? Dating's been around FOREVER!

Well . . . not *forever*. Joseph and Mary didn't actually *date*. We're not even sure George Washington dated. In other words, dating really hasn't been around forever . . . but it has been around long enough for it to *feel* as if it were always here.

No one dated in Bible times. When a guy reached marrying age, probably around fourteen or fifteen, his parents would help him find the right girl and they'd just get married.

Hundreds of years later, courtship was invented. A guy approached the father of the girl he wanted to court and asked his permission. The whole intent of courtship was to see whether this girl was the person he wanted to marry. In other words, one went *into* the relationship thinking about marriage. The courtship was a public thing; private, solo dates were unheard of. The guy came to the girl's home, spent time with her family, and hung out in the parlor. She'd have dinner with *his* family, hang out in *his* parlor. . . .

But things have changed, haven't they? Teens usually don't marry at age fourteen or fifteen anymore. No one's in a hurry to plow the fields, harvest a crop, and hang out at Grandma's eating cherry pie.

In today's society, by the time you're ready to date, you're also involved in piano lessons, football practice, Bible study, youth group activities, and band tryouts. In other words, you still have a lot of fun, teen-type stuff to do. There's no hurry to settle down and find a mate. But the *desire* to be with the opposite sex is as strong as it was in the 1800s when you *could* have married young. So what do you do?

You begin dating. But not with the firm intention of actually *marrying* the person you're attracted to. Again, no one gets married at fourteen today. You begin dating simply to spend time with the opposite sex and learn how to relate to him or her.

Even though this whole book is about dating, what we're really talking about here is spending time with the opposite sex. Having fun. Deepening your friendship.

◄ DATING DEFINED ►

As you get older, the reasons for dating change. When you're in college or a college graduate, you begin to date specifically to find a lifetime partner. *So why not just wait till college to begin dating?*

Many people do. And as mentioned earlier, that's normal. It's also normal to start at an earlier age (with your parents' permission) simply to develop your social skills and to become good friends with the opposite sex.

Some of the Old, Some of the New

Even though things have changed, there are still a few good ideas from the olden days we ought to think about implementing in our dating lives *today*.

Respect the 'rents.

Respect for your date's parents will go a looooong way. Spend some time getting to know them. Ask some fun questions about *their* dating lives. Listen to their answers. Here are a few ways to get to know your date's parents better:

1. Invite yourself over for dinner. Say, "Could I bring over a bucket of chicken this Friday night? And maybe a couple of side orders of baked beans or corn on the cob?" I don't know of any parents in the world who would turn *that* down. Chances are, they'll probably offer to make the veggie dish. Great! You're "in"

now. Might as well go for broke. Ask your date if you can come over an hour earlier so the two of you can make a chocolate cake.

2. Offer to help with a project around the house. Say, "Could I come over Saturday and mow the lawn for you?" Great idea . . . unless it's winter and the grass is dead, in which case you might want to offer to help wash the windows, organize a garage sale, paint a room, or wallpaper the den.

3. Spend time with your date's siblings. Say, "Let's take your little brother to the circus this Saturday." Great idea. This tells the parents you'll be in public (which is always a plus), and lets them know you care about the family.

4. Phone Mom and Dad. If you're going to be late getting back, stop and make a phone call. Explain where you are and why you're running late. Your date's parents will respect you a lot more if you're honest and you let them know *ahead of time* that you ran into a snag . . . instead of speeding back, dropping off your date, and speeding home with no explanation.

5. Plan Group Dates. We'll give you some great group-dating ideas later in the book, but for now seriously consider doing fun things in public. Why? Because, if you're dating someone to get to know them better, then do things that will really help you get to know them better! One of the best ways to do that is by staying away from tempting situations. The more you do things with other people around, the better you learn how to relate—*really* relate to your date.

6. Get Permission from the Parents. OK, this one's a little old-fashioned, but it'll go a long way with your date's parents. Even before asking someone out for a

date, consider asking her mom or dad if they'd mind if you asked her out. Yeah, it'll feel weird at first. But it won't take long, and you'll feel like you're friends with her *parents* as well as with *her!* You'll get a double blessing. Think about it.

It All Comes Down To . . .

Whether or not you decide to implement some of these ideas, dating all comes down to respect. The more you involve your date's family and other people, the faster you'll gain the respect of those around you.

Remember: dating is supposed to be FUN! So relax, have a great time, and enjoy the bazillion loopy suggestions in this book!

"One of the first things girls notice about a guy is whether or not he knows how to respect women. Opening the door should just be an automatic thing. Taking care of situations and having a plan is also impressive. When I'm going out with a guy and he says, 'Well, what do you want to do? Where do you want to go?' I want to say, 'Back home!' I enjoy being with a man who knows where he's going."

Cindy Morgan, Christian singer

TIPS FOR STEADY DATERS

▼▼▼▼▼▼▼▼▼▼▼▼▼▼▼▼▼▼▼▼▼▼▼▼▼▼▼▼▼▼

Though we've got quite a few ideas for first-time daters, much of the book is best used for those who are in a "dating relationship." That is, you're spending time building a friendship with one person on an exclusive basis (you're "going together," hopefully with the approval of your folks).

Why do we want to help these types? Here's the progression we've seen happen a million times.

1. You hear through the grapevine that someone of the opposite sex would go out with you if asked. Or the relationship begins without anyone else's prompting. You're attracted to him/her, you have some courage and confidence, so you make the first move. "Wanna go to the game together this Friday, then out for pizza?"

2. You and the other person enjoy yourself on the first date, and try for a second.

3. Then a third, fourth, and fifth. Before you know it, neither of you is terribly interested in spending time with anyone else. You're in deep "like"; so you talk about your relationship and decide that, for now, you'll date only each other. Sometimes the guy will even give the girl a friendship ring, a necklace, or a dead frog—anything that communicates a higher level of commitment.

4. You continue to date, but soon the same old stuff gets boring. And we're not just talking about the same fast-food restaurants. Holding hands is cool, but goodnight kisses are slightly more fun. After a few months—or weeks with some teens—longer kisses in the car or on the couch just aren't cuttin' it anymore on the excitement scale. Your mind begins to tell your hands to go exploring.

5. Given the wrong time and wrong circumstances, all of a sudden, true love hasn't waited—true lust has taken over.

This book isn't meant to address the whole dating and sex issue (our other book, *What Hollywood Won't Tell You About Sex, Love and Dating* does that). But it's easy to predict the progression—actually, regression—of what occurs when you're bored, you've got time on your hands, and you and your date are alone.

What you need are IDEAS!

That's what this book is about. Ideas to have fun, ideas to deepen a friendship, and ideas that will put the relationship through potentially stressful

circumstances to help you get to know "the real them." That's what you'll find in these pages.

If your goal in a long-term dating relationship is to move toward more sexual involvement, what you're now holding won't help. But if your goal is to do the dating thing right—from the very start—hey, you've made a smart investment.

GOOFY THINGS NEVER TO DO OR SAY ON A DATE

▬▬▬▬▬▬▬▬▬▬▬▬
▼▼▼▼▼▼▼▼▼▼▼▼▼▼▼▼▼▼▼▼▼▼▼▼▼▼▼▼▼

- Try to act cool by spitting out the window . . . forgetting it's still rolled up.

- Stick your worn-out gum to the underside of your date's leg instead of the chair in a movie before you start eating popcorn.

- Sing to the songs on the radio if you're tone deaf.

- Tell your date they're tone deaf if they're singing to the songs on the radio (unless it's the tenth date).

- Burp out the theme to *Star Trek* (Guys, we don't care how good you are at this—don't do it!)

◄ **GOOFY THINGS NEVER TO DO OR SAY**

- [ ] Talk about *anything* related to the bathroom.
- [ ] Mention anything about "funny smells," (unless it's the ninth date).
- [ ] Talk about how much fun you used to have with your old boyfriend/girl-friend.
- [ ] Mention other people you hope to date one day.
- [ ] Ask if your date's hair color is natural.
- [ ] Talk about your uncle Ed, who's currently serving time in the state penitentiary.
- [ ] Ask how much money his/her parents make.
- [ ] Pop your knuckles in all ten fingers (unless it's the thirty-sixth date).
- [ ] Pop your knuckles in all ten toes (unless you're married).
- [ ] Ask if the golden necklace your date is wearing is actually *real* gold or just a cheap imitation.
- [ ] Discuss terminal illnesses, especially if they're in your family.
- [ ] Wear slacks that are so tight they could split with the slightest movement.
- [ ] Apologize for the way you look or smell.
- [ ] Apologize for the way your *date* looks or smells.
- [ ] Order the most expensive thing on the menu.

ON A DATE ►

WHILE YOU WAIT

☐ Comment about your date's driving: "Watch it . . . watch it . . . there's a red light three blocks away! Hey, where'd you get your driver's license? Outta the Cracker Jacks box?"

☐ Comment about your date's car: "I saw a car just like this at the junk yard last week."

☐ Ask how long he/she usually dates someone before breaking up.

☐ Mention anything about deodorant.

ABSOLUTE MUSTS **FOR** GUYS

- Meet her parents, let them know what your schedule will be for the evening, and especially what time you'll be home.
- Open her door.
- Make sure the temperature is comfortable for her in the car.
- Keep your hands to yourself. Ask permission to hold her hand if you think you'd like to.
- Don't change the plans for the evening unless you get her permission, then call her folks.
- Always keep quarters in the ashtray in case you need to make emergency phone calls.
- Check the spare.

▣ Carry plenty of money. You don't need to go overboard and bring along a bunch of traveler's checks or credit cards; but *make sure* you have enough for the entire evening, plus a little extra in case of emergency.

▣ Check the gas tank and make sure you have plenty of gasoline *before* you leave.

▣ Be flexible. If your date isn't enjoying the evening, ask if there's anything you can do to make things go better.

▣ Make sure your date is comfortable. For example, if she's shivering, turn up your car heater or loan her your jacket. If you're ice skating and she seems miserable, ask if she'd be more comfortable in a warmer place.

▣ Make sure she knows how to dress for the evening. For example, if you're going to a football game, she'll probably dress differently than if you're going to the musical *Cats*. If you're not clear on what the evening will entail, she'll be upset with *you*.

▣ Strive to create a positive memory for your date. Make a memory she'll enjoy sharing with her friends and a memory she'll want to relive again . . . with *you*.

▣ Talk. Nothing is more frustrating for a girl than going out with a guy who can't put two words together. Ask your dad (better yet, ask your mom) to help you make a list of questions if you have to, but be prepared to carry on a conversation.

ABSOLUTE MUSTS FOR GIRLS

- When a guy asks you on a date, find out exactly what the schedule will be.
- Dress appropriately. If he's taking you to a nice restaurant, then to a play, don't wear jeans. If you're unsure how to dress, ask him what *he's* wearing or what would be appropriate for the evening.
- Whatever you wear, *don't* wear it too short, too tight, or too low. Why tempt the guy you're with? Encourage him to be a gentleman by the way *you* dress.
- Carry some extra money. Even though your date may be paying for everything, always be prepared for an emergency.
- When eating out, try to wait and see what he's ordering, then you'll

know a good ballpark figure for your own dinner. (If he orders soup and a salad, it probably wouldn't be wise for you to order a steak and baked potato.)

Be considerate. Realize the guy is probably nervous. He may say something stupid or try to get your attention in an off-the-wall manner. Be patient and realize a first date is not really an accurate gauge for a continuing relationship. Determine to have a good time.

Give him a chance to be a gentleman. For example, don't jump out the door as soon as the engine is turned off. Give him time to open your door.

Don't initiate touching. Many girls make the mistake of reaching for their date's hand or touching him during a conversation. This can give the guy mixed signals that he doesn't need.

Create a positive memory for him, one he'll want to relive again . . . with *you.*

Realize a guy will likely run out of things to talk about after the first fifteen minutes. Have a stockpile of questions to ask, or topics to talk about, when the conversation starts to wane.

When the relationship is starting to get more serious, make sure your guy knows exactly what your standards are. He can't read your mind, and if things aren't spelled out *exactly,* there's a chance he'll see how far he can get.

REJECT LINES NEVER TO USE

The job of coming up with "reject lines" is mainly a girl problem. Guys just aren't smart enough to know what to say if a girl asks them out and they're not interested. If they don't want to go, they're likely to do something insensitive like say, "I'll meet you there," then not show up.

The job isn't easy, but you'll make it a lot tougher than it has to be if you ever try to use any of the following lines:

- "Sorry, but I'd rather wait by the phone for Roger to call. He has a nicer car."

- "That's my Pinochle night with my aunts and uncles. . . . The next night? Well, that's when I usually help my little brother with his Legos. . . . Next week? I'm not sure, but I do recall my mom saying something about a family getaway in order to tour the kitty litter factory in the next county. May I call you?"

|||||||||||||||||||||||||||||||

⬜ "Ha, Ha, Ha. You're soooo funny. I can see why everyone thinks you're the funniest guy at school. See you in class on Monday." (You've probably just destroyed a guy who's spent a month trying to drum up the courage to ask you out.)

⬛ "Your acne problem wants to make me gag every time I look at you. Call me after you've seen a dermatologist for about a year." (A definite *huh-uh*.)

🔲 "Would we be going out in public together?"

🔳 Anything that goes like, "I'd rather_____ than go out with you."

⬜ "You mean *together?* As in you pick me up and actually *take* me somewhere? You and me???"

⬛ "Let me pray about it first."

🔲 "Have *you* prayed about this?"

🔳 "That's my night to help the librarian re-catalog the non-fiction books."

⬜ "My dad needs help cleaning out the attic, and obviously I'm the one who should pitch in."

⬛ "You're not my type."

🔲 "I think Dad's supposed to teach me how to change the oil in our family car that night."

- "I'm not really looking for a relationship right now." (He didn't ask for a relationship—just one evening!)
- "That's my night to study my Sunday school lesson. I always like to be prepared in case the teacher asks me a question."
- "You're kidding!"
- "Why???"
- "I'm not that kind of girl."
- "I promised Mom I'd help her reorganize the freezer."
- "What would people think?"
- "Hung zeep oh chop!" (Never a good time to pretend you're foreign.)
- "AHHH! No way!"
- Anything that starts with "You're sweet, but . . ."

"Guys, when you're on a date, ask yourself this question: 'If this were my sister and a guy was dating her, would I want me for my sister's boyfriend?'"

Pam Thum, Christian singer

PEOPLE YOU'D NEVER THINK OF DATING

You may already be dating someone, or have an idea of the type of person you'd like to date. You may even have your eyes peeled for that certain someone. We'd like to offer a few suggestions, though, about whom you date. You could even say that, well . . . we'd like to set you up.

That's impossible! you're thinking. *You don't even KNOW me!*

You're right. But we'd *still* like to set you up, because we really, really, really believe you'll benefit from going out with the following people at least once. Now, granted, they're probably not people you'd naturally think of when trying to decide who to go out with. But trust us, OK?

Your Parents

Hold on! Before you turn the page . . . just hear us out, will you?

For Girls Only

Girls, your dad obviously knows *something* about dating—he married your mom, right? Ask him if the two of you can spend an evening to talk. Spend some time asking him questions about guys, dating, and marriage. Here are a few questions to get you started:

- How long did you and Mom date before you got married?
- How did you meet?
- How did you know you were in love?
- What's the most memorable date you've ever had? What made it so outstanding?
- What's the most embarrassing date you've ever had?
- What attracted you to Mom?
- What's my best quality?
- Is there anything in my character I can be working on to improve?

WHILE YOU WAIT▶

- What will guys think is the most attractive quality about me?
- How can I help guys see Jesus in me?

For Guys Only

Guys, why not treat your mom to an evening out? Who better than your mom can tell you how women want to be treated by a man? Make up a list of questions to discuss during your time together. Here are a few to get you started:

- What are a few things guys do that turn girls off the most?
- What are some things guys can do that girls always appreciate?
- How did you and Dad meet?
- What attracted you to him?
- Do you see any of Dad's qualities in me?
- What qualities in me will girls be attracted to the most?
- What should I be working on to improve?
- What's your most memorable date? What made it so special?
- What's the most embarrassing date you've ever had?
- How can I establish godly dating relationships?

"The best date I've ever had was with my mom!" says Brian Barrett, Christian contemporary singer. I was on spring break, and for some reason, the rest of the family wasn't able to go; so my mother and I went to Disney World in Orlando, Florida. We had the time of our lives!

"We rode a lot of rides and looked around at all the neat shops—we even got rained on. I remember buying some little candies that were coated with a chocolate powder—they tasted like they were covered with dirt. In fact, I couldn't help but inhale some of the powdery chocolate up my nose when I started eating them. There I was, standing among all these tourists coughing and gagging because I'd snorted chocolate powder up my nose. It was embarrassing, but funny. I'll never forget it!"

Your Youth Pastor and Wife

You may be from a church that doesn't have a youth pastor on staff. Then spend an evening with your youth leader, Sunday school teacher or senior pastor and wife. (Make sure you go out with the pastor *and* spouse. Trust us, it'll look better. For example: girls, it wouldn't be wise for you to approach your married youth minister and say, "Can we spend the evening together? Just the two of us?" Go ahead and include the both of them. More fun!)

Again, make up a list of questions ahead of time, but here are a few to get you started.

How did you two meet?

- How did you know the other was the one you were to marry?
- Did you pray together on dates?
- How did you establish a godly dating relationship?
- Do you have any regrets about your dating life together?
- What was the strongest quality about your dating relationship?
- What's the strongest quality in your marriage?
- What part of marriage do you have to work the hardest at?
- How can I be a fun date?

Yourself

Believe it or not, *you* are the perfect date for *you!* Pop some corn or order a pizza and treat yourself to an evening alone while thinking seriously about your dating life. You may want to keep a journal or notebook of your thoughts. Start with the following questions, then add some more of your own.

- What are four specific qualities I want to see in the person I date?
- What specific qualities do I want others to see in me?
- If I were a member of the opposite sex, what about me would make me want to ask myself out?
- What are some specific hedges or safeguards I can create to protect my integrity?

- What kinds of entertainment will I *not* be involved in with my date?
- What actions have I seen from others that I want to make sure I don't repeat?

God

Because God knows you better than anyone in the whole world (and loves you more than anyone else), spend some quality time with Him to pray about your dating life. Again, here are a few items to get you started. Add more of your own and record your discoveries in a journal or notebook for future reference.

- How can I be a reflection of Jesus during my dates?
- How can I prepare myself spiritually before leaving on a date?
- How can I help my date be all God wants him/her to be?

A Couple of Saints

Find an elderly couple in your church who have been married for a long time and treat them to a special evening. Here are some questions you might want to add to your own list:

- What's the most important ingredient in your marriage?
- What has made your marriage so successful all these years?

WHILE YOU WAIT▼

▪ What role does God play in your marriage?

▪ What's the best advice you've ever received regarding your marital commitment?

▪ What advice would you give someone just beginning a dating relationship?

"A great date for me is to be with someone who's involved in some kind of ministry. That's my world, therefore, what I have most in common with someone. The second thing is someone with a good sense of humor."

Carman, Christian artist

TRUE LOVE WAITS

An Unforgettable Memory

A few weeks before her thirteenth birthday, Shauna Menefee of Abernathy, Texas, started dropping some hints to her parents about what she wanted. "A ring would be really cool," she told them.

They not only picked up on her hint, but drove her to the jewelry store and let *her* pick out the ring!

"It was really fun," Shauna remembers. "We looked at several, but I kept coming back to this pretty gold one. It had a heart in the middle that really caught my eye."

Shauna's parents purchased the ring, wrapped it and kept it hidden for two weeks. Right before her thirteenth birthday, her dad surprised her.

"Shauna, your thirteenth birthday is really special," he said. "Your mom and I want to treat you to a nice dinner at a classy restaurant. We'll get all dressed up and make a memory we'll never forget."

The Big Day Finally Arrives

After Shauna was presented with a beautiful corsage, she and her parents headed out for an evening of fine dining.

"After we placed our dinner order, my mom pulled out several birthday gifts," Shauna says. "I unwrapped a new belt, some hair bows, a book I had been wanting . . . but no ring."

Their steaks arrived, and through the course of the meal, her dad started talking about the ring.

"Shauna, you picked out a beautiful ring for your thirteenth birthday. And though you didn't know this, it's a very *special* ring."

"We're going to call it a chastity ring," her mom said.

"In the next few years you'll date a variety of young men," her dad continued, "and your mom and I want you to uphold the dating standards we've helped you establish. We expect you to maintain your sexual purity until marriage."

"Shauna," her mom said, "let this ring be a symbol of your virginity. It will represent your commitment to God to remain abstinent until you're married."

As Shauna opened the beautifully wrapped package, she couldn't help but feel the depth and seriousness of the gift.

"I had already decided to maintain my sexual purity," she says. "I'm a Christian—it's not an option. I'm determined to follow God's will for my life.

"But as I slipped this special ring on my finger, it deepened my heart's desire to become all that God wants me to be."

Committing *Now* and for the *Future*

Shauna's fifteen years old now. "It'll still be awhile before I actually start dating," she says. "But you know what? Someday when I'm out with a guy and he reaches for my hand, I'm going to feel my ring against his flesh. That's a pretty powerful reminder of my commitment.

"And even now, when I catch myself daydreaming in class, I start fiddling with my ring—you know, twisting it round and round. And I smile deep inside, knowing that someday I'll present this very ring to my husband on our wedding night as a symbol of the most important gift I can give him—my virginity.

"I realize I may fall in and out of love several times before I finally commit to the man God wants me to marry. This ring is not just a symbol of virginity; it's also a reminder not to do *anything* on a date that I'll regret. So my ring is a constant reminder to take everything that happens during a date seriously."

But Everyone's Doing It!

It seems as if we're bombarded with messages of sexual "freedom" in ads, TV, and movies. But really—is *everyone* doing it?

"I realize just by watching the news that lots of young people are involved in sexual relationships," Shauna says. "The pregnancy rate for unwed teen moms continues to skyrocket, as do sexually transmitted diseases.

"But to say 'everybody's doing it' just isn't real life. *I'm* not doing it. My closest friends aren't doing it. NOT EVERYONE IS DOING IT! And to fall for that lie is just plain stupid. God has a much higher calling on our lives."

Sometimes . . .
> *Sex*
> *Sounds a lot like love.*
> *But it's not.*
> *"I want you"*
> > *Doesn't mean*

▲ TRUE LOVE WAITS ▶

"I want to give my life to you."
"I need you"
    Isn't the same as
"I will be here for you."
"You're gorgeous"
    Doesn't mean
"I love you for who you are."
"Look how happy we are"
    Isn't the same as
"I will be content with you 50 years from now."
"It feels good"
    Doesn't mean
"I want you to feel good about yourself
    when it's all over."
"I'll be gentle"
    Isn't the same as
"I care about your feelings."
"Everybody's doing it"
    Doesn't mean
"I want us to do it God's way."
"It's so good, I want it now"
    Isn't the same as
"It's so good, I'm willing to wait for it."

Sex
  Is not the same as
LOVE
  No matter
    How similar
  They sound.
(By Ruth Senter, reprinted from *Campus Life* with permission.)

What about you? Are you determined to wait? It's not necessary that you have a physical reminder, like a ring, to keep your commitment fresh. Your promise to God is the most important factor.

But if you *do* want a physical reminder, there are other things besides a ring that you can use. Maybe you've signed a "True Love Waits" card. If so, you're probably carrying it in your wallet or purse. Ever think about having it laminated? It'll last longer, and it's inexpensive. If you haven't signed one, check out the back of this book.

Or maybe you've heard of the Love Pendant. You can order one from Focus on the Family (P.O. Box 35500, Colorado Springs, CO 80935-3550) for $20. It's a 14-karat gold-filled design with a sparkling cubic zirconia surrounded by three hearts and three question marks. The question? "If I do this, will it show love for God?

For others? For myself?" (The chain is not included.)

Many parents have presented their sons and daughters with gold key chains, watches, or necklaces to serve as chastity reminders.

How Can I Get My Parents to Give Me a Chastity Symbol?

Talk with your mom and dad about your desire to follow God's will for your life. The perfect time to do this would be during a "date"—a special evening out—with just you and your folks. Tell them then you want to keep your virginity until marriage.

Explain what you've read, or show them this chapter, and ask if they would consider giving you a chastity symbol as a special gift.

If they choose not to be a part of this venture, then see if you can line up a few extra odd jobs and purchase your own chastity symbol.

But above all, remember: it's not the *physical* item that's important, but rather your *spiritual* commitment to your heavenly Father.

BETWEEN YOUR FIFTH ●AND● TENTH ●SOLO● DATES

Polaroid Moments

Find an old Polaroid camera (ask a relative, neighbor, or friends from church or school if you don't have one). Call around to a few larger drug stores to see who has film. It'll probably cost between $5 and $7.

The film box comes in rolls of about ten. You can divide up who gets in which photos any way you want, but it might be fun to do three or four of each of you, then try to find someone to take the rest.

Finding weird places to take them is what will make it fun.

- Standing next to the statue in the middle of town.
- Pretending you're pumping gas in the other person's ear.
- Having the guy hold up a girl's outfit in a department store like he's interested in buying it.
- Putting a LOUD tie on the girl and having her wear a plaid sport coat.
- One of you who climbed to the top of a tree.
- Trying on sunglasses . . . four at a time!

Be creative. Do something wacky and out of the ordinary, something that goes totally against your normal personality.

While you're going to all of these places that you wouldn't normally go on a date, talk about some off-the-wall things you've done in your life. Let your date see a side of you that perhaps only your best friends have seen.

Creative Option #1: Instead of using a Polaroid, spend a few extra dollars and buy one of those disposable cameras. It's not as fast—and you will have to pay for developing—but it's just as handy.

Creative Option #2: If you don't like photographs (and one of you is already making over $20,000 a year), hire a fast sketch artist at between $50 and $100 per hour to go around with you to draw you in all of the fun places you want to remember.

WHILE YOU WAIT▼

You Don't Have to Live in Hollywood

If you live in Southern California, getting tickets to TV tapings is usually no big deal. They happen on Thursday and Friday nights, and with a little pre-planning, you can see whatever show you want.

But how about in your town? Well, if there's a TV station within a fifty-mile radius, you might have the makings of a creative date. Local stations do their own programming. Even if it's watching your local news celebrities read their lines from the teleprompter, it's still pretty good entertainment. No, you wouldn't plan your whole evening around it, but it makes for a unique diversion from the ordinary.

Creative Option #1: Call up your favorite radio station and ask if you can bring your date in some Friday or Saturday night for a look-see. Tell them you won't stay long, but you think it would be fun to see how they do what they do. Some will say no, but most disc jockeys working Friday nights would welcome the company. As long as you're not obnoxious and don't ask them to play your favorite song six times while you're there, you should be able to kill an hour or so. Hey, TV and radio don't make bad careers—and the Lord needs more of His kids in these media. You might even be able to get a few questions answered about education requirements and pay scales while you're there!

Create Your Own Pizza

This isn't just another pizza. Buy the dough and sauce from the grocery store, but *all other ingredients* must be obtained by asking for them! That's right. Call your friends, go door-to-door, whatever it takes, but no fair *buying* any ingredients.

Once you have the ingredients, use them to create a face or name or some kind of special design on the pizza. And for memories? Take a few photos of your creation!

Grab the Paint!

Start your own business. Paint addresses on the curbs outside people's homes. Shop together for paint and stencils, then charge $3 a curb. You'll be surprised how much you can make in just one day!

Visit the Local Animal Shelter

If you're really feeling generous, purchase a lonely pet and give it to a child who would love to have it. (Better check with his parents first!) Even if you choose not to purchase a pet, you'll enjoy seeing the variety of animals waiting to be loved. You may even want to make a list of the ones you like the best and try to find a home for some of them after you leave.

Create Your Own Holiday

Either make up a new holiday or celebrate a non-publicized one. Check out a book called *Chase's Annual Events* that's filled with fun, off-the-wall holidays. Once you've decided on a specific day to celebrate, create your own special cards and mail or deliver them to friends.

You may even want to highlight your celebration by having a PARTY! Be as creative as you can . . . after all, it's *your* special holiday. Here are a few you may not be aware of:

- February 24 is French Fry Day.
- March 1 is Peanut Butter Lover's Day.
- March 12-18 is Fun Mail Week.
- The whole month of April is National Humor Month. (And you thought those April Fool's jokes were only good for one day out of the year!)
- April 4 is National Reading a Road Map Day. (How 'bout sending out party announcements on the back of old maps?)
- May 8 is No Socks Day.
- June 6 is National Yo-Yo Day.
- July 16 is National Ice Cream Day. (Try making some homemade ice cream and celebrate with several friends!)

 December 26 is National Whiner's Day. (Ever thought of having a whiner's party?)

Make Up a Mystery

Create your own mystery together and bring in friends to help solve it. You may even want to hand out specific clues to each couple who comes to the mystery event.

Plan a Garage Sale

Make some money together by organizing a garage sale. If you don't have enough items between the two of you to sell, collect additional things from your church or neighborhood. Use the money for:

 A contribution to your church's youth group

 The local animal shelter

 A favorite charity

 The missions program at your church

 Buying fun gifts for everyone in both of your families

WHILE YOU WAIT ▼

Create Your Own Sitcom

Tired of the same ol' same ol' on TV? Then write your own sitcom! Who knows? You may even be able to sell it. (And we're talking BIG BUCKS if you *do!* Non-union freelance writers—that's *you*—can make around $10,000 for one script!)

What're You Sayin'?

Consider signing up for a foreign language class together. Not only will it be fun studying, but imagine what others will think when you start conversing with each other in a language they won't be able to understand!

And the Winner Is . . .

Every April the Gospel Music Association presents the annual Dove awards to outstanding Christian artists. Why not have your own Dove awards party? Invite several friends, have them dress fancy or dress as their favorite artist or group, and watch the event together.

Get your date to help you plan the evening, make refreshments, and cast ballots from your friends as to who they think will receive specific awards.

Head to the Airport!

You can have a *lot* of fun at your local airport. Wear an outfit made out of leopard-like material or something that looks as if it came from the 1930s. Assign different personalities to each other. For instance, your personality may have an English accent and be extremely dainty. Your date's personality might be a macho man with a southern accent.

Act as if you know someone getting off the plane: "Uncle Bob!" Or act as if the two of you are having a welcome home reunion: "Oh, Sharon! You've been gone forever. The kids really missed you!"

Or simply sit and watch people . . . but make up your own rules for whom you're watching. For example, you can't get up until you've counted ten bald men, or five pregnant women, or six babies, etc.

Get Set . . . GO!

Volunteer to help at a Special Olympics competition. Ask several friends or other couples to join you. Bring a camera and take photos of your memorable time helping others.

Get Out the Sponge

Have a car wash—just the two of you—then put all the money in a "dating fund" for future fun times together. Who knows? You just might bring in enough money to pay for that special Valentine's banquet you both want to attend. Or that concert with $25 admission tickets.

Picnics in the Park

Dress up or dress down, but going out for lunch or dinner to a park—especially one with tons of little kids—can be a blast. Both of you need to bring something for the meal. Plus, you'll need a huge blanket to sit on. While you're eating, talk about which kid best describes you when you were a little tyke.

You may even want to start the date *before* the picnic by *preparing* for the picnic. Why not go to your local department store and purchase a couple of kids' lunch pails? Then fill them with goodies and head to your favorite spot!

Try a New Sport

Sure, you could go outside and shoot some baskets, throw the football, or toss the frisbee . . . but here are a few ideas to stretch your horizons:

- horseshoes
- racquetball
- croquet
- indoor volleyball
- volleyball with the lights out (we dare you)
- shuffleboard
- pavement darts (it is *really* tough to get those babies to stick!)
- fly fishing
- bee fishing (not!)
- dock fishing
- bank fishing
- bridge fishing
- ten-story building fishing (open the window first)

Feed the Ducks

Go to the supermarket and buy a loaf of day-old bread. Find a park or a lake where there is waterfowl, and you've just created a memory. Why? Because it won't take long before you have big, mean geese chasing you to get your bread. Also, you'll probably have to take off your shoes when you're done to clean off all the geese "land mines" you stepped in.

Home Cookin'

Instead of heading out to a restaurant for dinner, take the $10 to $20 you would have spent and go to the store to buy what you would have ordered. Do you like steak and shrimp? You can get a nice steak and a dozen or so shrimp for about $8. How about calzone? All it takes is some dough, pizza-type ingredients, a pre-heated oven, and some red sauce and you can make this Italian favorite almost as good as the best place in town.

Bumping into each other in the kitchen while making stuff you've never made before is fun. Even if your food doesn't turn out "restaurant quality," it will more than likely be edible.

Even if you think you don't know how to make anything, don't let that stop you. Ask your mom or dad exactly how to make a certain dish (take notes), get the ingredients together, and make the evening special. Because you're staying home instead of going out, your folks may even keep little brothers and sisters out of the way. Who knows, maybe even the whole family will stay in another part of the house so you can have a little privacy, too.

Grocery Shop

Volunteer to do one (or both) of your moms a HUGE favor. Do the grocery shopping for the week. We know, it sounds a little domestic for a date—and one of your friends may see you shopping together and wonder what's going on—but if you're secure enough, it'll be fun.

Simply make sure you have a complete list of what's needed, enough cash to buy whatever is necessary, get in the car and go.

Pet Stores

Nearly every big mall has a store with fish, snakes, cats, mice, parrots, iguanas, gerbils, hamsters, bunnies, and of course, dogs. They're almost like a free zoo or aquarium—you can spend a good hour walking around and talking about which animals you like and which are gross.

Red Light

Take turns making turns.

Whenever you come to a red light, one of you must say whether to turn left or right. You alternate after each light. (If there's a one way street, our strong advice is to go the direction the traffic is going.) The fun part happens when you land in a (safe) part of town you've never been in. Then you have to find your way home! (Be smart. Always carry a map in the car!)

NEVER...

- [ ] Take your date to the county landfill to find good stuff that rich people have thrown away.
- [ ] Wash your dirty underwear—or fold clean ones—while you're killing time watching TV.
- [ ] Talk about relatives in mental institutions.
- [ ] Take food off of the girl's plate unless you know for 100-percent proof-positive she's absolutely done eating (then ask).
- [ ] Take food off of a guy's plate even if you know for 100-percent proof-positive he's absolutely done eating (don't even ask).
- [ ] Try to impress him (or her) by inhaling a spaghetti noodle through your nose and into your mouth.

- Talk about what kind of dishes you want for your wedding on your first ten or twenty dates.
- Lie.
- Talk about the medication you're taking.
- Ask about medication your date has taken.
- Talk about your dating failures.
- Ask about your *date's* failures.
- Write your own wedding vows, then try them out on your date.
- Remove anything from your nose while your date is looking.
- Remove anything from your *date's* nose . . . even if *no one* is looking.
- Gargle the "Star Spangled Banner" with Pepsi.
- Gargle.
- Show pictures of your last boy/girlfriend.
- Talk about something you really don't know anything about.
- Assume your date knows what you're thinking or feeling.
- Share your trigonometry homework.
- Throw anything at your date . . . unless it's a Frisbee or a softball.
- Play with fire (or anything that can *start* a fire).

▲ NEVER... ►

WHILE YOU WAIT ▶

- Take your date to a bee farm.
- Show your baby pictures.
- Try to guess your date's weight or measurements.
- *Mention* your date's weight or measurements.
- Two-time your date.
- Try to "fix" or straighten your date's hair or clothing.
- Ask if your date's parents have a prison record. (You'll find out . . . eventually.)
- Show your date any scars or scabs you might have.
- Ask to see your *date's* scabs or scars.
- Talk about marriage.
- Mention any injuries you received or inflicted on your last date.

"GOING TOGETHER" DATES

Have Some Class

During the summertime—or even during the evenings—there are specialty classes you can take that might be fun.

- Pottery and ceramics
- Woodworking
- Auto mechanics
- Bible classes
- Art
- Music lessons

- Photography
- Drama
- Creative writing
- Ballooning
- Scuba diving

Check the schedules for your local YMCA or community college. Yes, it takes a few more dollars and a little more commitment but even if the relationship ends, you've picked up a few things you didn't know about before.

Discover Their Past

Spend an evening or a day at the other person's house, looking through all of their old photo albums from when they were kids. Discover where the other used to live, where they've been on vacation, which relatives they have good memories of, how many kids used to come to their birthday parties, etc. It may be the most enlightening evening you'll ever spend with them.

If they have home movies or videos of when they were growing up, look at them another time—*after* you've looked through their pictures. The reason: It's probably been so long since they viewed them that they won't want to talk, they'll just want to watch and listen. This is fine, but it doesn't meet the goal of actually speaking to each other.

Car Shopping

Everyone dreams about what kind of car they'd own if they had the money. If your town has an autoplex—a place where a bunch of car dealerships are right next to each other—spend an evening kicking tires and looking at the upholstery. If you dress up to look like you're rich, the salesman may even let you test drive that sports car you've been drooling over the last two years.

Design Your Future Home

Okay, we know you're probably not going to marry this person, but if you could design your dream home, what would it look like? Get some graph paper and scale the drawing to size. Then for fun, ask your dad how much a house like this would actually cost!

Memory Lane

If you really want to get to know someone—and one or both of you has lived in the same town for a lot of years—take a drive together. Go past old schools, churches, neighborhoods, playgrounds, ball fields, or houses you used to live in and tell a few stories. You'll find memories that you haven't thought about in years flooding your head.

Will everything be a happy memory? Probably not. But that's OK. Hearing the other recall things that weren't so pleasant is the perfect way to really get to know them. This is also a pretty good Saturday morning or rainy day date.

Dining a la Abnormal

Tired of eating at home and restaurants? Are picnics in the park too passe? Then it's time to get abnormal! Pack some food and find some place "out of the ordinary" to eat it at:

- Inside an elevator that's going up and down
- A neighborhood tree house
- On a fenced in bridge over a busy highway
- In the far corner of the public library (no chips or carrots allowed)
- At your high school baseball field, whether any team is playing or not. Home plate is always nice.
- At the edge of the eighteenth green of your local public golf course
- On the top roof of your flat roof house
- On the top roof of your neighbor's flat roof house (ask first)
- In a bowling alley

WHILE YOU WAIT ▶

- ▣ Tailgate in the parking lot of a shopping mall; then go in for dessert
- ▣ Next to a river or lake
- ▣ The highest point in town
- ▣ In the middle of a corn field
- ▣ In the middle of a cow pasture
- ▣ In the middle of a subway station (except in New York)
- ▣ At the train depot
- ▣ Outside a factory at quitting time (be sure to hide your food as best you can)
- ▣ On a ski lift in the middle of summer
- ▣ On a huge inner tube in the middle of winter
- ▣ Any restaurant parking area
- ▣ A nearby highway rest stop
- ▣ In the middle section of a well lit parking lot where the lights are low.
- ▣ At the bus station
- ▣ In your church parking lot

Store-Bought Stuff

You can have a blast with cheap stuff you can get from a department store:

- Marbles
- Silly string
- Play-doh
- Whiffle ball
- Pick-up sticks
- Twister
- Puzzles
- Jacks
- Models
- Cheap airplanes (balsa wood, styrofoam or plastic, it doesn't matter)
- Miniature games you're familiar with that are now called "travel games"

A Few More Ideas

- Organize a bake sale together. Bake all the goodies together, then run the sale!

WHILE YOU WAIT▶

Make candles together, then deliver them as fun gifts. For something extra, add some old cologne or perfume to scent each one!

Pack four sack lunches and treat your date's parents to a picnic in the park.

Perform random acts of kindness together. Decide for an entire month that your dates will consist of doing kind things for others. Here are a few suggestions:

Challenge your friends to participate in some random acts of kindness for one week. Then invite them over for a "Kindness Party" and allow everyone to share the kind things others have done for them, and what they've done for others.

Visit your pastor's house and announce that the two of you are there to make a surprise cleaning. Vacuum, dust, and do the laundry for them.

Order a pizza and take it to an elderly couple in your church or neighborhood who don't get to dine out much.

Fill a couple of gas cans and deliver them to someone so they won't have to fill their tanks this week.

Take a case of Pepsi to someone in your neighborhood.

Make some small purchases at your local variety store, then let the person in line behind you go in front of you.

If you live in a city with a toll booth, pay for the car behind you.

▫ Write an appreciative note to a former teacher or coach and thank them for the positive impact they had on your life.

▫ Buy a few carnations and deliver them to someone on your church staff. Thank them for their ministry and the job they do.

▫ Renew someone's newspaper subscription for another year.

▫ Purchase a $5 or $10 gift certificate from a local restaurant and deliver it to a police officer.

▫ Make some hot apple cider and deliver cups of it to local merchants.

▫ Buy some inexpensive mugs from your local craft store and fill them with candy corn and peanuts. Then you can deliver them to people who are on your church roll but have missed a few Sundays.

▫ Take some nuts or seed and spread them in the park during the winter for hungry birds.

▫ Canvas your neighborhood and pick up all the trash.

▫ Volunteer to spend Saturday morning helping check in books at your local library.

▫ Offer to read books during "Story Time" at your local library. If they don't have a "Story Time," ask if you and your date can start one.

▫ Purchase some leftover, brightly-colored adhesive paper from a local print shop—the kind that bumper stickers are made out of. Create your own

stickers and pass them out to children at the mall, in your neighborhood, at the hospital, or in your church.

☐ Get a list of missionaries from your church and send them care packages.

☐ Give your church custodian a break and volunteer to clean your church for one week.

☐ Gather up all the clothing you no longer wear and deliver it to Goodwill or the Salvation Army.

☐ Create your own greeting cards and send them to at least twenty people in your class that you don't know well.

☐ Get permission from City Hall to plant a tree (or a plant) in the local park.

☐ Spend a half hour collecting all the stray shopping carts from the grocery store parking lot and return them to the store.

☐ Write a appreciation notes to parents of ten of your friends.

☐ Volunteer to help out in your church office. Type the bulletin, create a new bulletin board, help with the newsletter, etc.

☐ Wash and wax your dad's car.

☐ Stand outside the entrance of a busy store and hold the door open for people.

☐ Shovel snow off your neighbor's driveway. (Depending on the time of year.)

- Mow your neighbor's lawn. (Depending on the time of year.)
- Make dinner for your entire family. Even if it's hot dogs or frozen dinners, your thoughtfulness will be appreciated.
- Volunteer to help out in the nursery this Sunday at church.
- Did you watch something uplifting on TV in the past week? Write a letter of appreciation to the network.
- Rake and bag the leaves from someone's yard.

"GOING TOGETHER"

DATES ▶

SATURDAY MORNING DATES

To break up the monotony of the same old Friday night dates, stay home with your family once in a while, go to bed early, then get up around 7 A.M. and drive someplace to have a nice breakfast (Money Saving Hint: Most girls aren't as hungry in the mornings, so they won't eat as much. You'll save big-time!) After getting your fill of cholesterol, grease, and caffeine, try these ideas:

Discover Little League

Even if you don't have any friends or relatives who qualify, take an hour and go watch a T-ball game. Cheer for the kids like they were all your nephews or nieces. If you really want to make a few friends, bring sodas or popsicles for the kids to enjoy at the end of the game.

67

Other options are basketball leagues at YMCAs and neighborhood grade schools, or touch football. Wherever kids are found, you'll find a few laughs and a few new things to talk about—such as what sports you played when you were in grade school, how good you were, what your coaches were like, if your parents were like the loud parents you notice at the game, etc.

The Bookmeisters

Go to your local bookstore and peruse the aisles. Pick out books that, if money were no option, you'd buy and . . .

    ▣ probably let sit on your shelf.

    ▣ might read the first few chapters.

    ▣ would more than likely eventually get around to finishing.

    ▣ wouldn't put down until they were done.

(Girls: This is really the perfect way to find out if your guy has any *real* interest in college or learning. If he keeps going back to the big picture books on cars, planes, war, or sports—or the cartoon books—you'll have a hint of what the future holds with him. If he doesn't have an interest in books, he probably won't have much to talk about once the initial attraction to you wears off—except cars, planes, war, sports, and the cartoon channel.)

(Guys: This is the perfect way to find out if your date is in touch with reality. If she heads over to the romance section and shows you thirty-seven novels she's *already* read, you've got a girl who likely isn't in touch with reality. Her expectations about guys and relationships are going to be so out of whack, it will take years to bring her to the truth that most guys, at best, are only *occasionally* sensitive and romantic.)

This idea could be used with any evening date, as well as for Saturday morning.

Shoot an Arrow

Most towns have an archery range that will rent equipment and target time. This is a fairly sophisticated sport, but fun. It's not as loud as gun practice, and you don't get those invisible powder burns on your hands.

Bake Something

It doesn't matter which house you choose, plan ahead to get the right ingredients, make sure the kitchen won't be in use, then bake stuff for a few hours.

- Cookies—dozens of them! But don't eat them all yourself. Find out if there's a Sunday school class the next day that could use them.

- A cake—big, beautiful, and bizarre. Do elaborate icing designs, make it look like Texas, whatever. Just try not to make a two-layer chocolate

cake. Too predictable, too boring and it won't take long to do it.

- Pizzas for the family dinner.
- Sub sandwiches for the family lunch.
- A few different kinds of muffins for Sunday morning breakfast.

Kid's Day

Flash back a few years and do a bunch of kid stuff for the entire morning. Start by purchasing some brand-new crayons and a couple of coloring books. Grab some children's games from your closet (or borrow from a child in your neighborhood: CandyLand, Chutes and Ladders, Mouse Trap, Chinese Checkers, etc.) Next, head to your local library. Check out ten children's books and head to the park. Take turns reading to each other, then spend some time coloring and sharing favorite childhood memories. Take time to play the games you brought; and at the end of your Saturday morning date, exchange completed coloring books with each other to keep as a memento of your flashback time.

Go-Karting

If your city doesn't offer go-karts for rent, how 'bout making your own? Visit the lumber yard together, purchase the materials you'll need, head to the junk yard

and find some wheels (small motor is optional), grab some paint and create your own vehicle!

Garage Sales

They're fun. They're inexpensive. And they're all over the place! Check your newspaper for garage sales in your area and begin the morning with $5 each. See who can make the most purchases by noon. You may be surprised at some of the great deals you'll find!

Batting Cages

Even if you aren't any good at baseball, it's fun to try your swing in a batting cage. It's not expensive, and it's a creative way to spend some time together doing something a little different.

Driving the Golf Range

Visit your local golf course, not to golf, but to rent a golf cart for the morning. Drive around the range, pick up a few stray balls (make sure someone's not looking for them!), bring some orange juice and muffins and have breakfast on the greens (if you can actually get away with this, write and let us know).

Create a Music Video

Select a favorite song and borrow a video camera for a day. Then head to town and create a video you can tie in with a school project, or for extra credit, or use in one of your youth group meetings.

Tickle the Ivories

Why not sign up for Saturday morning piano lessons together? Or if you already play the piano, try another instrument: drums, guitar, accordion, kazoo. After six months of lessons, give a private recital for each other.

Warehouse Food

Many larger towns feature a few huge warehouse-type food stores where you have to buy sixteen of everything to save twenty-three cents. About 11 A.M. on Saturdays, however, most start hawking food at the corner of every aisle. You can practically eat an entire meal just by going around taste-testing everything. (Hint: Push a cart around with a few items in it to make it look like you're there to do more than eat.)

GREAT GROUP DATES

Soda Tasting

You've heard of wine tasting? How about organizing a soda, or mineral water, or Snapple tasting? Instead of spending $15 to $20 on a movie, invite a few friends over and spend the cash on some exotic, non-alcoholic drinks you've never tried before. There's a few ways to do it:

- have each person rate what they like best so you can choose an overall winner;
- hide the labels and have the participants guess what they're drinking;
- buy several of each type of drink (Cola, Root Beer, Lemon Lime, Orange, etc.), and compare which has the best taste.

You'll need to buy small cups (like bathroom cups) along with having plenty of ice.

Creative Option #1: You can do the same with gourmet ice creams, popcorn, coffee, or Pepperidge Farm cookies (Greg's favorite). Just walk the aisles at your local supermarket and pick out things you can buy that would be a kick to taste. This could be something you do with a few other couples on a monthly basis—or better yet, your family might want to get in on it, which means they might spring for whatever it is you're tasting.

Creative Option #2: While you're tasting or sipping, play a few of your parent's old records—you know, those large black discs that look like big CDs. If their music was bad, try watching a couple of Godzilla or old Jerry Lewis or Don Knotts movies on video. If you just want background noise so you can talk, play your favorite Christian music.

Airports

Most towns and cities have at least one major airport within driving distance. After you've saved up to pay for parking and a soda—the only two essentials that will cost you—go to the various parts of the terminal, sit and observe.

The best game to play is "guess."

■ Guess who the people standing by the gate are waiting for to get off the plane. For example: Older moms or dads, children, husbands, wives, relatives they'd rather not see, business associates, girlfriends, boyfriends (check the ring fingers).

- Go to the baggage claim area and guess how much luggage they have to take home with them. (I guess you'd have to be pretty bored to do this one, but hey, you try writing a book with a million ideas in it.)
- See how many men go into the restroom as soon as they de-plane.

Super-Sized Popsicle

It'll take a *really* good-sized group to eat *this* masterpiece! Grab a bunch of friends and head to the store for a few purchases: 30-gallon hard plastic trash can, tons of Kool-Aid, and a big 2 x 4 from the lumberyard.

Thoroughly clean the trash can, then mix up the Kool-Aid. Pour it into the trash container, place the 2 x 4 in the middle, then head to the local ice plant or freezing unit. For a small fee, they'll let you freeze your giant Popsicle overnight. Be ready to do some serious munching the next day!

Gladiators

It'll take a lot of planning, but the fun and memories will last a lifetime! Plan a human gladiator party with your date or a few other couples, then invite thirty to

forty of your friends. You'll want to think up several events of your own, but here are a few to get you started:

Pillow Power. Get a sawhorse and put foam rubber or a lot of loose hay underneath. Allow two people to stand on top of the sawhorse, each armed with an old bed pillow. At the sound of the signal, each starts whopping the other with his pillow. First person off the sawhorse loses.

Human Velcro. It'll take a while to make, but the laughs will linger! Find an old mattress—the bigger, the better—and line it with velcro. Next, find a large jumpsuit (could probably be found at a Goodwill store) and sew velcro material on the outside. Place the velcroed mattress against a wall with a mini-trampoline, the kind used for exercising, about six feet in front of the mattress.

Only one person can participate at a time because he will put the velcro-jumpsuit on over his clothing. At the signal, he'll run toward the mattress, jump off the mini-tramp and "stick" himself to the wall. Have someone with a stopwatch standing nearby. The longer he stays "stuck" on the wall, the more points he receives.

Human Bowling. This works best in the summer when you want a break from the heat. Spread out a large piece of plastic tarp and place a water hose on top. At the end of the tarp, place ten small plastic trash cans, symbolizing bowling pins. At the signal, the first contestant runs toward the tarp and slides into the plastic cans. Points are given for how many pins are knocked down.

Dinner Party

You know how adults are constantly doing church potlucks, Christmas potlucks, and potlucks for no good reason other than to get together around food? Well, you may be sick of them by now, mainly because it's more like "try your luck," but they're still a pretty cool invention.

If you're a guy, suggest a dinner party to a girl you know pretty well and see if she and few other girls would organize it. Though it's not too macho for guys to organize a potluck, it's perfectly OK for you to bring stuff (but please, for everyone's sake, ask your mom to make whatever you bring).

If you're a girl, all you have to do is mention food to a bunch of guys and you're sure to draw a crowd. For optimum success, be sure to include the four basic food groups: pizza, soda, chips, and candy.

Creative Option #1: Believe it or not, "fonduing" really is pretty fun. That's when you dig out your parents old fondue set and ask them what to put in it. What you'll hear are ideas like heated cheese and bread, heated chocolate and marshmallows, heated oil and steak or fish, etc. It's a slow way to eat, but by the time the evening's through, you've usually eaten enough.

Creative Option #2: Tell each person to bring pizza ingredients and bake up four or more different kinds. One person supplies the crust—make it or buy it—the others bring the pepperoni, Canadian bacon, pineapple, mushrooms. . . oh yeah, grated cheese, olives, anchovies, sausage, chocolate chips, etc.

Creative Option #3: Do a Mexican, Italian, Chinese, Greek, or Southern food potluck. Breakfast for dinner potlucks are a blast, cheap, and easy (instead of a brunch, it's called a brinner).

Creative Option #4: Buy a six-foot roll that you can cut to make deli sandwiches. Have everyone bring their favorite deli sandwich fixin's, create a masterpiece—then eat it!

Scavenger Hunts

Let's say you can round up twelve people and three cars. Agree to meet back in one hour, and see who can go out and collect the most matchbooks. No, you can't go to the grocery store to buy them, you've got to hit restaurants. Develop a point system for single-wide, double-wide, wooden, specific colors, whatever. After you're done, someone can either start a collection, or you can go out in the back patio (use the barbecue or cement, please) and have a bonfire. Bring a few marsh-mallows, too. Though we've never actually tried this one, we think that if you get a matchbook going by placing some fire underneath it, the rest will light up one at a time. The affect could look pretty cool (but make sure you've got a fire extin-guisher handy).

Creative Options: Business cards, restaurant napkins or place mats, cookies from neighbors and friends, candy from dentist offices, soda cans or bottles—different. Just use your imagination.

WHILE YOU WAIT ▼

Nick-at-Night

For two weeks before a group get-together, videotape short segments of different old shows on Nickelodeon ("Dick Van Dyke," "Mary Tyler Moore," etc.) The idea is to have every main character that was popular in the '50s, '60s, and '70s on the tape.

One major goal, of course, is to become as fluent in black-and-white TV as your parents so you don't keep losing to them in those trivia board games.

If you want to add some intellectual stimulation to an otherwise mindless evening, create a written test. As each character appears on the screen, "contestants" must write down the actor's stage name and their real name. Sample: The real name of the man who played the Professor on *Gilligan's Island* is Russell Johnson. If they know the answer, they get two points (and a slap on the knuckles for watching *waaaaaay* too much TV). You, of course, have control of the remote control when everyone wants more time to think. The winning person or team gets an incredible prize: they get to keep the tape.

Creative Ideas #1—12: Do the same in whatever category would interest your group the most: Saturday morning cartoons (or any cartoons); Sunday TV preachers (the late-night ones are just as "good"); prime-time sitcoms; Atlanta Braves baseball players; local or national newscasters (yawn!); weather channel hosts (double yawn!); A & E *Biography* personalities; talk show hosts (nah, that's too easy); WWF personalities (If you don't know who they are . . . good!); new and old *Star Trek* characters; *Pro Bowlers Tour* guys (triple yawn); animals and insects from *National Geographic* shows (now, *this* has potential!).

Whiffle Ball

Remember when you were little, you'd play whiffle baseball until dark? Sure, it's been a long time since you picked up that six-ounce bat; but if you have about seven guys and seven girls, you'll have a blast. Here are some new rules:

It's girls against the guys. The girls get to use that big, fat, red plastic bat and a small ball with no holes in it. The guys have to use that skinny yellow bat and a real whiffle ball (one with holes in it). If the score still gets too lopsided, guys have to bat left-handed.

If you want to mix up the sexes, that's OK, too. Guys get overhand pitches, girls get underhand.

(If you hate the fact that Greg is assuming here that guys are better than girls, play normal.—Susie)

(Hey, I'm not trying to be a chauvinist, just a realist. Besides, if it's high schoolers who are playing, the guys have finally caught up to the girls in size. I suppose that if it's junior highers who are playing, it's OK to give the guys the big, red bat.—Greg)

Puzzle Race

If you like puzzles, but don't like taking three weeks to put one together, try a different twist. Divide up into teams of two. Go to a department store and purchase four puzzles with between 250 and 500 pieces apiece (they cost between $2 and $4). Set up two or more tables close to each other, then put all of the pieces face up. When you're ready . . . go! See which two people (or three or four) can put their puzzle together the fastest. Then trade teams and try again.

Creative Option #1: If you don't mind being around each other's parents or siblings, get them involved in the race if you can't find a bunch of friends. (*Guys versus girls always proves that guys are much more analytical and perceptive when it comes to complex things like puzzles.*—Greg)

(*And it also proves that guys are so insecure that they have to compete about everything just to prove to themselves they have value.*—Susie)

Coupon It

You and another couple check the newspaper and junk mail for a week or two and see who can come up with the best deal for eating out. Whether it's chicken, pizza, burgers, or Romanian goulash, it'll be cool to see who can save the most money on a meal for four.

Scavenger Hunt

Make sure you check with your folks on this one. No use getting the whole neighborhood calling your home to complain. If you've never done this before, here's how it works.

Make a list of things you can get by going to twenty or so houses: cookie, a can of tuna, an old sock, a joker from a deck of cards, a plastic fork, etc. Nonsense stuff is the best. Then, make two lists, one for each team. Set a time limit, talk about courtesy rules (no running through yards, saying please and thank you), and then when everyone gets back, compare stories.

Creative Idea #1: Try a scavenger hunt with a purpose. Go door-to-door for food. That's right, instead of getting junk you're just going to throw away, call a local food bank (your church might have one) to see exactly what and what not to get. If each team has a pickup to put food in, you can end up getting a lot of food. It's for a great cause, people are more likely to give, and you'll feel like you really accomplished something.

The winning team scores the most boxes of food. What does the winner get? Maybe the parents of the host home will spring for pizza or ice cream.

WHILE YOU WAIT ▼

Fast Food Progressive Date

If you've got eight people or more, you may need a few cars. After you've got the wheels, you need to live in a town that has more than a Dairy Queen. Now that you're in the right town, do you have between $6 and $8?

Criteria met? If so, proceed.

Drive to a fast food joint with a salad bar and get one pass, salad only plate. Make it less than $1.50.

Next, head off to a fast food fish place where they sell chowder. Again, don't spend more than $1.50 on a cup.

Still hungry? Though the girls may not be, the guys are! Hit some place with a gourmet entree. You know, stuff like a McLean Deluxe, Arby's Roasted Cheddar, the Colonel's extra crispy chicken, Dominos pan pizza for one, whatever. Depending on how much you have left, try not to spend more than $2 to $3.

Full yet? Well, drive around town and waste some gas (um, car fuel) to make room for dessert. When you're hungry again, look for a cheap ice cream place. If you've got a few extra dollars—the girls will, guys, believe us—you could even head to Denny's or someplace that sells pies.

You've just killed about three hours having outrageously clean fun, you've fed your face, and you're so full all you want to do is go home and go to sleep. Hey, this could be the PERFECT date!

|||||||||||||||||||||||||||||||||||||||||

Creative Idea #1: Instead of being progressive, try *regressive*. That's right, do dessert first, then the entree, soup, salad, and appetizers.

Creative Idea #2: Do all of your ordering from the drive-thru, and all of your eating in the car. Bring plenty of napkins—better yet, towels—to clean up clothes and upholstery.

Bad Movie Night

Go to your local video store and rent a few 99-cent movies that are so bad, they'll be guaranteed to be hilarious. Anything with Godzilla, giant insects, the Three Stooges, black and white sci-fi flicks, Abbott and Costello, Jerry Lewis, or a Japanese film with subtitles will be a kick. Have someone man the remote to fast-forward through the slow parts. You can watch up to six movies in one evening!

CELEBRITIES' WORST DATES

Terry Jones, Point of Grace

The absolute worst date of my life was with the man I ended up marrying! It was our first date, and he wanted to take me to a Bobby Brown concert. I'm really not crazy about his music, but I agreed to go.

We sat in the nose bleed section, and the concert was really rowdy. A guy in front of us was smoking pot and it smelled so bad, we finally had to move.

Chris went into the bathroom, and I waited outside for him. The crowds were so rowdy and the people were really weird. This guy came up to me and started pulling me down the hall.

When Chris came out of the men's room and saw me heading down the hall with another guy, he just thought that we knew each other and didn't pay any attention to it . . . until I started screaming for him. When he realized what was going on, *he* began reacting and almost got in a fight with this weird guy that neither of us knew!

Things were so hectic that we lost track of time and I had to call my dorm mom because we were out past curfew. It was a fiasco! We walked out to the car to leave and this gang of guys approached us and one of them grabbed my necklace right off my neck!

So Chris stormed over to them (Like what? He's gonna fight thirteen guys?) to try to get it back for me, but the police pulled up. The guy was pinned to the ground and I had to identify him before we could leave.

Finally, we got to the car and a dog jumped out of nowhere right in front of us! Chris squealed the tires, slammed on the brakes, and we almost had a wreck just trying to avoid the animal!

We finally started back to the campus, but noticed bright lights behind us. It was the police! They pulled us over for speeding. Chris explained the entire evening to the officer, and luckily he let us go without a ticket.

When we were only three minutes from the school, Chris's car started smoking. It was so bad we couldn't even see in front of us. We got out, but he said since it was still running, he'd have to go ahead and drive it back to his dorm. He told me to run back to *my* dorm, since I was already past curfew.

With all we'd been through that night, I was scared to death. I couldn't believe he

wanted me to run back *alone*. But by the time I arrived at my door, he was waiting for me. He had run all the way from *his* dorm just to say he was sorry.

Pam Thum, Contemporary Christian Artist

It was the first time I'd gone out with this guy, and he took me to an amusement park. He had his camera with him and wanted to take pictures. I was wearing a sweat suit, and he wanted to go down the log ride. I usually don't mind getting wet, but it was really chilly that day, and I didn't especially want my picture taken in a wet sweat suit.

But I went anyway, and whoever was supposed to take our picture messed up, so my date said, "We'll have to go down again."

I was *shivering*. But he just kept on at me, so I finally agreed to go on it one more time. By the time we climbed out of the log, I was *drenched*. So I said, "It's really cold. Do you think we could go back to the car so I could get my other clothes to change into?"

But he just wouldn't listen. Instead, he dragged me to the next thing on his list—which was an air-conditioned show. The music was super-loud, and I was sitting there totally miserable and thinking *never in a million years do I want to see THIS guy again!* He was going to town with the music, totally oblivious to the fact that I was catching pneumonia and hating it more and more every minute I was with him.

The guy was totally insensitive and had no understanding or compassion that I was shivering.

Denise Jones, Point of Grace

I went out with this guy in college who didn't have a car, so I had to drive. We went to a high school football game. Not only did I have to pay for the gas to get there, but it was two hours away. He never took me anywhere for dinner, so I finally stopped at McDonald's and had to buy my own. I couldn't *wait* to get home!

Gary Chapman, Contemporary Christian Artist

My worst date ever was also the best date I ever had. I had picked Amy Grant up for a date that was quickly going from bad to worse. Ironically, I had already asked Amy's father for her hand in marriage, and had planned on proposing to her that night.

We got into an argument the moment I picked her up, and we fought all through dinner. Finally, carrying a load of laundry and walking Amy back to her dorm, I figured that at this point if she said yes to my proposal, we were *bound* to succeed. So I proposed right there—in the parking lot behind "Steak and Egg" restaurant.

WHILE YOU WAIT►

Amy said, "Shouldn't we pray about this?" And I said, "Yes, but I still need an answer."

And as everyone knows . . . she said yes!

Cindy Morgan, Christian Singer

My worst date was with a guy named Scott. I was working at a men's clothing store in Knoxville, Tennessee. He'd come in and bring me roses and say stuff like, "Hey, Baby." Even though he was annoying, he was still nice—and cute—so I went out with him once.

He had these really big dice hanging from the mirror inside his car, and he had *carpet* on the dashboard. He was playing this amazingly loud acid-rock music that I absolutely hated, and had this incense thing that smelled like the beach. It was so gross! On top of all that, his muffler was torn off, so the car was really loud. It wasn't that it was a bad *car,* it was just everything he'd *done* to it.

I smelled like coconut oil when I got out of the car. We got to this comedy club and he *didn't* open my door, so I just got out myself. I was starving when we got inside, and all he got were a few munchies—cheese sticks or something like that. Because he worked in this building, he got everything for half price. The whole date cost him $3.50! He was a total dweeb.

It was obvious I wanted to go home, so he started the car . . . and of course, the beach odor came again. He finally pulled up in front of my house and he just stared at me. I thought, *If you think you're going to kiss me, you're out of your mind.*

He said, "Don't you want to give me a kiss?"

I said, "No!"

Then he went, "OK, see ya." And dropped me off at the curb.

Heather Floyd, Point of Grace

There was this guy at Ouachita Bible College that I went out with. He was a freshman and sat in front of me in a class we had together. The guy was real funny—the cowboy kind. And he was really short.

Well, we went to the movies together at the campus theater. It was awful. I felt so dumb because there was such a difference in our heights! We got popcorn and Cokes, and my arm was on the arm rest between the seats. He decided to hold my hand, and my arm was so much longer than his, that it was hanging over the end of the arm rest and back under!

Andy Landis, Contemporary Christian Artist

We were both in high school, and I went out with a guy who said he just wanted to get to know me. So we went to the movies. Well, first of all, he was late picking

me up and didn't even bother to apologize. Second, his car was absolutely *gross* inside.

Then he drove really, really fast—which scared me to death. I asked him to drive slower but he just laughed. I couldn't *wait* to get home, but after the movie he wanted to stop for ice cream. I agreed, but told him we couldn't stay long, because I needed to get home early.

Other friends were at the restaurant, and he kept trying to hold my hand and put his arm around me—which made me totally uncomfortable. He also tried to get me to smoke and drink—to which I said no.

Finally, I said I *had* to go—and when he tried to kiss me goodnight—I said no to *that*, too. I felt like I spent the entire evening saying no!

Looking back, I guess it was good practice. "No" is really a good word to know how to say.

Jody Davis, Guitarist for the Newsboys

My worst date reads like a B-movie from the early '80s. I picked up my prom date, forgot the flowers, and she ditched me about one-fourth of the way through the evening. There *was* ONE good thing that happened, though. The band called me from the dance floor to sing and play on the final song of the night. It was really cool!

Shelly Phillips, Point of Grace

I went out with this really sweet guy in college, but it just wasn't meant to be. He had the worst breath! I mean, it was so bad I couldn't even look him in the face. At the end of the night I literally *ran* in the house to keep him from trying to kiss me!

Kevin Mills, Newsboys' Bass Player

I had only recently broken up with a girlfriend of three years; and for the first half of my first date with someone else, I called her by my old girlfriend's name until she finally corrected me.

Pam Thum

One of my most embarrassing dates was at a wedding. The reception was really fancy, and of course everyone was all dressed up. Wouldn't you know it—I got the hiccups! And when *I* hiccup, it's not a cute, little dainty thing. It's more of a snort.

My date took me through the receiving line to meet everyone, and it was awful. I'd stick out my hand to greet them and go, "Hi, I'm Pam. *Snort*. Nice to meet you."

WHILE YOU WAIT►

Creative Ways to Say, "I LIKE YOU!"

Want to make a special memory for the guy/girl you're dating? Use the following ideas to get you started, then add some of your own.

- Using kids' bathtub paint, write "I like you!" on his/her locker, front porch, windshield, or vinyl notebook. (It washes right off and won't damage anything.)

- Purchase an inexpensive fanny pack, have his/her name embroidered on the front, and fill it with favorite candy.

- Make and send your own greeting card, using pictures from magazines or newspapers that remind you of favorite things.

- Borrow a video camera and create your own video filled with "You're special" messages.

- Buy a child's lunch pail and fill it with his/her favorite munchies.

- Have your picture taken in one of those inexpensive photo booths at the mall (four photos for approximately $1), and hold up different messages written on cardboard for each photo: "You're terrific!" "I like you!" "You're special," "You're my favorite person to be with!" etc.

- Buy an inexpensive photo frame and decorate it yourself. Then frame a fun photo of the two of you together.
- Make a cassette tape of his/her favorite songs, with fun messages from *you* between each song.
- Hide a stuffed animal in his/her locker or on the front porch with a sign that reads, "You're the best!"
- Dress funny and deliver your own singing telegram.
- Ask someone *else* to dress up funny—someone he/she doesn't know—and have *them* deliver your singing telegram!

DATES AROUND ● THE ● HOLIDAYS

Make Ornaments

- For homemade ornaments mix four cups of flour, one cup of salt, one-and-a-half cups water, and food coloring (optional; add to water before mixing). Mix all ingredients together. Squish dough with hands until completely blended. The dough should be firm and moist, not sticky or crumbly. Bake at 325 degrees for two hours or until completely hardened. Put some glue around the edges, throw on some glitter—and you've got instant ornaments.

- Old *Reader's Digests* make great Christmas trees. Simply fold the top of every page all the way to the middle, then fold the bottom up to the middle, too. After you've folded every page, glue two of them together. Now, get a can of gold or silver spray paint, and cover the whole thing with color. You've got a pretty cool-looking ornament that you can set on fire when Christmas is over.

☐ Go to a hobby store and purchase a couple dozen styrofoam balls. Next, buy a bunch of glitter, beads, pins and stuff, and make your own round-type ornaments for the tree.

☐ String popcorn.

☐ Make a chain out of red and green construction paper.

☐ Buy a couple of packages of twinkling lights, find a big piece of ply-wood, make a star pattern with a pencil, put nails in the points of the star, string the lights (ending with the plug at the bottom), and you've got a star to light up the neighborhood.

☐ Try the same thing, except pound two boards together to make a cross. String the lights up and down, back and forth, and plug it in.

Creative Idea #1: Help an elderly neighbor to put up a few lights around his/her house. Then offer to come around after New Year's to help take them down.

Group Caroling

If your church youth group doesn't organize group caroling, call about twenty of your close personal friends—whether they can sing or not—and bless the

neighborhood with songs of the season. Who knows, you might even score some cookies and hot chocolate!

Creative Idea #1: Go to elderly shut-ins from your church and carol outside their home. Or, call ahead, then go to a nursing home and put on a thirty-minute concert. The smiles and tears will be awesome.

Serve Together

Get up early on Thanksgiving or Christmas Day and go to the nearest mission or homeless shelter. Call ahead to make sure they need volunteers and ask what you can bring and what time to be there. If you work from 7 A.M. to 1 P.M., you'll still have plenty of time to spend with your family the rest of the day.

On the way home, talk about the people you met. What were their lives like before they became homeless? What lessons did God teach you? How can you make serving a consistent part of your life?

Cook an After-Church Meal

Whether it's the Christmas Eve or Christmas Day service, most families like to eat after church. Why don't the two of you make the meal? What it will mean is being prepared before the end of the service so that when you get home, all you'll have to do is heat it up. It doesn't have to be fancy. A special type of

Sloppy Joes, chicken, spaghetti, TV dinners, pancakes with fruit . . . whatever everyone would like is fine. Doing this gives mom a break from always having to take care of *every* holiday meal, plus, as we've said before, getting in the kitchen is a teamwork activity. You have to communicate, do specific tasks, and coordinate your efforts to make it a success.

Cooking is also one of those dates that can test your patience. That is, you may or may not like what you see in the other person when it's over. Either way, you win. If it shows you the other person is a selfish jerk, it may be time to end the relationship. If the other person is really fun, and you work well together, well . . . that could be a good sign, too.

Christmas Lights

Nearly every city has one section of town where dozens of neighbors have gone *way* too far with their Christmas lights. There are literally hundreds of thousands of lights and displays on one street that almost make it seem like daylight. Find out where it is, wait until dark, then go look at it.

Creative Option: Drive around in your car looking at the lights, then stop someplace for hot chocolate when you're done. Talk about what you'll do when you have your own home.

Christmas Shopping, Sort Of

Yes, you need to shop, but how about a trip to a mall with one rule—you can't shop for anyone. What would you do? Observe folks. Are they having fun? Are they exasperated? Are they grumpy? Do they have a smile on their face? You can learn a lot about the person you're with simply by observing and talking about other people together. The reason: You find out how perceptive they are about human nature. If they can correctly identify *other* people's moods, they're probably pretty good at identifying yours. And if you can find someone sensitive enough to notice *your* mood swings—and respond accordingly—you may have the beginnings of something good.

It's a Wonderful Life

What Christmas would be complete if you didn't watch *It's A Wonderful Life* at least once? Guys, it's OK to cry at the end. You are hereby granted this special dispensation: *Males may cry at any point during this movie and retain their sense of cool and machismo at a later time without it being held against them.*

Creative Ideas: Miracle on 34th Street, The Gathering, Rudolph the Red-Nosed Reindeer, and *A Christmas Carol* (especially the one with George C. Scott as Scrooge), are all must-see holiday films.

"Guys, treat a girl as if you want to take care of her."

Cindy Morgan, Christian Singer

SUMMERTIME DATES

Bubble Mania

Remember getting those cheap soap bubble containers when you were a kid, the kind you used with the round goodies at the end that you blew into? When you're out driving around, stop and get some. Then go to a park, a school—or your house in the backyard if you don't want anyone to see—and see how long it takes to finish off the bottle. Who can make the largest bubble? Whose will fly the highest? Can you make so many so fast that the other person couldn't possibly pop them all before they hit the ground?

Creative Option: Spend a few extra dollars and get one of those huge bubble wands, a bigger supply of soap stuff, a container that can hold both of them, then really go bonkers with bubbles. What would be even more fun would be to take it

⟨ all to a park with kids and show a few how to do it. Along with getting these little ones really soapy, you'll put smiles on their faces.

Biking

Again, not real original, but you can make some great memories by biking. When I was in high school my girlfriend and I went biking along a busy road. During a lull in traffic, she road up beside me and bit my arm. I lost my balance (and composure) and we both went tumbling in the middle of the street. Had there been even one car driving by, both of us would have been killed. Instead, we lived to get married and have two kids. Now we have a memory we'll never forget.

Biking is great, but I don't recommend biting arms (just in case).

Canoeing

Many towns have lazy rivers or small lakes in which you can safely row a canoe about. Often you can rent a canoe or a small row boat for under $15. If your arms are strong enough to row, and if the wind isn't blowing, it can be a blast.

The good part about this date is you have each other as a captive audience. It's the perfect time to ask questions you've been dying to know about the other. The bad part is that you have each other as a captive audience. If you're not prepared to ask questions, tell stories, or talk about things you're interested in, the whole time you'll be wishing you could jump in the water and swim to shore. (Fact: Showing off your swimming prowess in this situation will unlikely win you any points.)

Blend Your Evening Away

Ever made a kiwi shake? How about a banana smoothie?

Set aside an evening to go to a store to buy some fruit, mix it with a small amount of ice cream or crushed ice, then sip your way to new thirst-quenching taste treats.

Try this: mix a few fresh blueberries and raspberries, one-third of a mango, a cup of milk and two tablespoons of Nestle's chocolate.

Or how about this: a whole canned pear, one-half cup of cottage cheese, one cup egg nog, a dash of peppermint, and two scoops of lime sherbet ice cream. Yum!

As you can see, the possibilities are endless!

(Whatever you try that actually tastes good, write it down and send it in to us. We may use your suggestion for our next book!)

Build a House

Whether or not you or your date have carpentry skills, committing a day or week to build or fix up a house for someone in need is a great way to check the "self-ish/selfless" meter. If you're with someone who wants only to do things that are

"entertaining," you've got a dud who'll likely be selfish in other areas, as well. Swinging a hammer or sloshing some paint together is the perfect test.

Creative Option #1: Find a neighborhood widow who needs help with her garden or yard work. If you don't know of any, call your church office—they'll know. For FREE, offer to spend a half-day doing things that need a strong back. By serving together you'll not only help another, you'll restore hope in the older generation that the younger generation isn't made up of a bunch of selfish pigs.

Creative Option #2: Before the yearly church work day is advertised, convince your date that a few hours pulling weeds, clipping bushes, or picking up trash around the church would be fun to do together.

Creative Option #3: Is there a neighborhood school, cemetery, or portion of your block that needs some tending to? Though you won't win an Eagle Scout award for doing something no one asked you to do, you'll feel better for making a piece of your world a little cleaner. And if you do it with someone you already enjoy spending time with, you win twice!

Go Fly a Kite

Kites don't have to be expensive, though a few high-tech ones can be. For a few dollars for a kite and string you can enjoy yourselves: putting the kite together (a formidable task by itself), getting it up in the air, and keeping it up.

What can you talk about?

- Family get-togethers you remember best.
- Your current best friends and why you like to spend time with them.
- Hobbies or collections you used to have as a kid.
- Colleges or careers you're considering.
- Your favorite musicians, groups, or singers.
- Concerts you've been to and what you thought of them.
- How and why you became a Christian.
- If you could change one thing about your family, what would it be?

CULTURED DATES

Museum Marathon

Look in the Yellow Pages under "museums." Take a whole Saturday and see how many you can hit. The object isn't to run through them—especially if you have to pay to get in—but to enjoy them to the degree you're able. If you don't like miniature doll museums, don't feel as if you have to look at every figurine.

Art Show Extravaganza

So you've never been to an art show. So what? Check the classifieds or the "entertainment" section in your Friday evening paper and go see a few. Believe it or not, seeing what some people can create with paint or pencil is fascinating. Talk to a few of the artists who are showing their work and find out where their ideas come from, how long it takes them to finish a piece, how much money they can make off a painting (hey, it can't hurt to ask), how does their new art compare with where they started, where did they go to school, were they the type of kid who always had a messy room.

A couple of these may be all you're able to handle; but like any other date, you'll find out something new about the person you're with. They may have absolutely *no* taste in art, or they may be a budding artist waiting to hear that they could become a great master. Plus, it's cheap. Rarely do art shows charge.

Creative Idea #1: Instead of going to an art show, create your own! Invest a few bucks in construction paper and water colors. Drive to a place in the city or the country, stop at a place particularly picturesque, take out all of your supplies, find something level and firm to paint on, and begin to make one "masterpiece" after another. (Don't forget to bring your dad's old T-shirts for smocks.)

It doesn't matter how good any of them are. And it doesn't matter if the girl can paint better than the guy, which she probably can. Just have fun, be creative, and be silly.

Creative Idea #2: This would also work perfectly for a rainy day date.

Creative Idea #3: Instead of trying to paint a picture freehand, buy a couple of those "paint-by-number" jobbies. You can still go to a picturesque place to paint. Just look up at the scenery, then paint, look up, paint. You'll feel just like Rembrandt!

Creative Idea #4: You say you don't like to get paint on your fingers? Try chalk. Buy a multitude of multi-colored chalk, find a huge cement slab to turn into a work of art, picture what you want to color in your mind, sketch it out first, then work as a team to complete the picture. (See group dates for another creative idea. Please note: This is not a good "rainy day" date.)

Creative Idea #5: Still want to try something else? How about charcoal. Crayons. Colored pencils. Magic Markers. Hey, you can even invade your little sister's room, round up all of this stuff, and blend it together (with water colors and chalk) into one incredible montage of color and styles. You'll probably start a trend so . . . trendy, you'll become world famous overnight. Art museums from throughout the world will be phoning in their six-figure bids to Christy's or Sotheby's Auction House to purchase your magnificent work of art.

Or . . . your mom may say, "That's nice," and then return to her needlepoint. Either way, you've done something you'll probably never do again. And if you're lucky, your dad will save it from the garbage can and put it in a box for you to look at twenty years from now.

Creative Idea #6: Get all the necessary stuff together and finger paint. Better yet, take it to a park where there are kids and let them finger paint (Note: bring enough smocks for everyone).

Dating Pointers from Point of Grace

Slow the Sizzle. "Never be in a hurry when it comes to relationships. It's too easy to think with your *heart* instead of your *head*. Take your time and develop a *friendship* with this person. After several dates, you'll know if he/she measures up to God's standards." *—Terry Lang*

Pursue Purity. "How can you remain sexually pure? By staying close to the One who is *ultimately* pure! By deepening your relationship with Him, you'll find that God will give you the strength to say no. The four of us made a decision back in junior high to remain sexually pure until marriage. And we STILL believe it's the wisest decision we've ever made!" *—Denise Jones*

Friday Family Fun. "It's totally cool to stay home on Friday or Saturday nights. This is a great way to 'date' your family. Use this time to get to know them better. Find out if your parents ever skipped school, were embarrassed by a member of the opposite sex, ever got yelled at by a teacher, etc." *—Terry Lang*

Treasure Your Ties. "Your family will always be there for you. Believe it or not, your school friends will eventually drift away. But your *family* is here for the long haul. So treat them like treasures." *—Shelley Phillips*

Find Forgiveness. "If you *have* let down your guard, don't fall for the lie that it's too late to change. You have a God who loves you! He wants to *forgive*

and *forget*. (Pretty powerful, huh?) DO consider talking with an adult, though, who can help you establish some healthy dating guidelines for the future." — *Denise Jones*

"I thought I was in love. My date took me to a New Year's Eve party on the river. There were tons of people and everyone was dancing. I had always wanted to do something really cool for New Year's Eve, and I'd never done anything like this! My sister and several good friends were with us—which made it even more special. We stayed up until midnight. It was really fun and romantic."

Heather Floyd, Point of Grace

DATES THAT TELL YOU A LOT

Having good, clean fun is important. But if all you ever do is pursue the next thrill, you'll become a shallow person. These next few date ideas may not qualify for "dates all your friends have got to try," but they have the potential to get you and your date talking about important stuff.

Hospital Visits

Many cities have Children's Hospitals, or at least a child's ward within the local hospital. Inside are kids with all sorts of ailments—everything from broken legs to cancer. Though they may look different from other kids, they're still kids. That means they like to do kid's stuff.

If they're girls, they'll like dolls, reading, talking, music, coloring, etc. If you're a girl reading this, you know what girls like to do.

If they're boys, they'll like sports cards, posters, toys . . . you know.

They just want to be normal and play. The problem: Their families can't spend *all* of their time at the hospital entertaining them or keeping them company. That's when these kids get lonely.

It's best to call ahead and ask for the hospital's policy on visitors to the children's ward. You may have to fill out a form or get interviewed, or they may just give you the best time to show up. Either way, going on this type of "date" together may be the best one you'll ever have. Who knows, you may even make a friend with someone who really needs one at this point in their life. Perhaps you'll stay in contact with them for a long time, like a big brother or big sister. Maybe you'll even have the chance to talk about your faith. Or maybe you'll just feel good that you spent an hour or more making someone else's day a little brighter.

Creative Idea #1: This takes a little more courage, and a little more compassion, but just as there are lonely kids in hospitals, there are lonely old folks in facilities for old folks. Again, call ahead to see what their rules are. Nursing homes may not be the best choice, depending on the type of ailments the residents may have. Some, as you know, do not have full possession of their mental faculties as they did in years previous.

Consider this option only if you're prepared to be consistent. That is, visiting older folks shouldn't be a one-time thing. They need—and want—someone consistent, at least once a month. Though the holidays may work for a one-time shot—and that's a good place to start—beginning at other times of the year is good, too.

Equipment needed: A heart of compassion, the ability to ask questions, the willingness to listen, and the knowledge that most of these folks are young at heart, but they're simply trapped in an old earthsuit. They're genuine people who have lived a full life. Actually, most are more interesting than you can ever imagine. The stories they can tell and the wisdom they can pass on may make this "date" a great experience you'll want to tell your friends about.

The reason this is a great date is because it's easier to do this with another person. That way, one of you won't have to carry the conversation alone.

Emergency Rooms

Bring a book or a few magazines to browse through (or homework), and spend a couple of hours in an emergency room at a busy hospital. Then observe.

Cemeteries

In the daylight, walk around and look at headstones in an old cemetery. Don't spend a ton of time there. Again, observe. If your date isn't hit by what you both see, his/her heart and soul may be a little too hardened by the world.

"I'd been in Australia and I hadn't seen my girlfriend, Summer, in six months, because she was in America. My work visa was waiting to be processed, and the date that I could leave had been postponed five times, which really upset both of us. When it finally did come through, I didn't let her know, and when I flew back to America, I had a friend pick me up at the airport. I bought flowers and a huge stuffed kangaroo—which I'd carried with me the entire 36-hour flight! My friend called Summer and asked her to come over and watch a video—just to cheer her up, and of course, I was there waiting for her. The best part of it was, when she got there, she was stunned to see me, and I asked her to marry me!"

Peter Furler, Drummer for the Newsboys

RAINY DAY DATES

What do you do when your plans get kyboshed by the weather? Well, you can either rely on the old standbys—dinner and a movie—or think about the dozens of options you have.

Board Games Aren't Boring

Every house is full of old games that don't get played anymore. The reason: You always played them with the same people, and you usually wore them out the first two months by playing them every other night. Pull a few out, and give them a second life. Which ones? While Clue, Monopoly, Life, Trivial Pursuit, Scrabble, and others are fun, the real fun ones are those that aren't too competitive: Chutes and Ladders, Candy Land, Monopoly Junior, Crazy Eights . . . you know, kids' games.

The goal isn't to win (guys!), but to do something together other than watch TV on the couch. Pop some corn, make some iced tea, and remember how fun it was to play these old games.

Creative Option #1: Go to Target or Wal-Mart and buy a new game. If a first-run movie and junk food cost $15 to $20, spend that on a game you've never played and pocket the change.

Creative Option #2: Get the parents in on it. Find a game that four people can play, make up teams (guys vs. girls is always fun), and take a couple of hours getting to know each other better over Monopoly.

Creative Option #3: Adults have been playing games forever, so that means they probably know a few you don't. Have them teach you something new to you but old to them.

Creative Option #4: Get a few other friends together (eight is ideal) and do a "card game marathon." Have everyone bring a few of their favorite games, take thirty minutes per game, keep score if you want, and trade teams to keep it from getting too competitive.

Guinness Book Guessing

Drive to a used bookstore and buy a *Guinness Book of World Records*. Take turns going through the pages, trying to get the other to guess the answers. "How much did the world's heaviest man weigh?" "What's the world record for the most chil-

dren born to one woman?" Hey, once you know all the answers, you can amaze your friends and family!

Play 12

Set up a miniature golf course throughout the house. Using large plastic cups set on their side for holes, make as many as you can. It might be 12, 6, or 18, it doesn't matter. Make sure you start upstairs first. It's tough (not to mention dangerous) to chip uphill indoors. Determine "par"—the number of shots it should take to get the ball in the cup—find a couple of putters (one would do), use different colored golf balls, and you've got yourself two hours of great entertainment. The only problem will be keeping little brothers and sisters from wanting to play every round with you.

Creative Option #1: If it's only sprinkling, get bundled up and set up a frisbee golf course outside. That's right, play frisbee golf in the rain!

Create a Trophy

There's a high probability that your parents and grandparents have a bunch of trophies stashed away. If they're no longer on display, that means they're in a box. Check with the owners first, then you and your date collect as many of these trophies as possible and start mixing and matching. Most are simple to take apart, and by changing tops, adding new levels, and putting on a new engraving, you've got the makings of a great gift.

Make a trophy for each of your best friends—or maybe even a parent or sibling. Don't sweat engraving, it doesn't cost much. You can say something ultra-creative like, "World's Best Friend," "America's Greatest Dad," "Detroit's Most Outstanding Mom" (make sure you're from Detroit). If you have little brothers or sisters, they would absolutely love this type of gift.

So you say there are no trophies in your house? Hey, you can buy used trophies, cheap, at garage sales, flea markets, estate sales, and thrift stores. Spend a few extra bucks and create an incredibly huge one that will be the center point of the entire room.

Redecorate!

Tired of your wallpaper? Wish your bedroom walls were a different color? Why not remodel a room together? Head to the local wallpaper/paint store to get some creative ideas, then get to work. (But ask your parents first!)

WHILE YOU WAIT ▼

Write the Right Way

Take advantage of the weather and stay inside! Get out some paper and write letters to your congressman, your senator, and the President (or if you're Canadian, the Prime Minister). Voice your feelings, your convictions, and your opinions. Also take time to share what you appreciate about what each of these people is doing.

Republican, Democrat, or Something Else?

Volunteer to help register people to vote. This may be available only at certain times during the year. Call the City Hall or your local government office to inquire about details.

What *IS* This?

Have a leftovers feast and eat everything (that's not moldy) in the fridge. It's an inexpensive date, and your mom will love you for cleaning out the refrigerator!

It's Rising . . . It's Falling

Buy $10 worth of stock together, then check your daily newspaper and mark the rise or fall of your investment.

Memorize Useless Stuff

OK, you're *really* bored. Go through the yellow pages and learn a few facts about your town. You'll be flabbergasted at the number of businesses that actually think they could make money. We live in a city of about 280,000. You'd think a city that size could support only about fifty pizza parlors. How many are there? Eighty-nine! Try lawyers. We have hundreds! How about doctors who specialize in various areas—podiatrists, obstetricians, gastroenterologists, etc. The number will amaze you.

Once you've collected all this semi-useless stuff by letting your fingers do the walking, you'll have tons of new facts you can use to stump everyone at the dinner table!

OLD STANDBYS

Hiking

OK, so hiking isn't too original, but we think old standbys can still be creative. Pack a lunch that will fit in a backpack, drive a few miles, and start walking. Heading off to a waterfall or the top of a mountain will be most memorable (don't forget a camera). Be sure to bring enough clothes for inclement weather. (Safety Hint: Some mountain regions have afternoon thunder or lightning storms, so go early.)

What can you talk about while you're on the trail?

- Biology teachers (always a great source of humorous stories).
- Biology partners (ditto).

How different it smells than the city.

Bees, mosquitoes, other miscellaneous insects, blisters, bears, low-flying birds, slugs on the trail, that green bush that looks a lot like poison oak but you're certain isn't, rocks that resemble states, clouds that resemble countries.

Every outdoor experience you can remember while growing up.

This particular date is especially fun with another couple. Reason: If someone sprains an ankle, there will be more people to help carry him/her back to the car. Plus, you can carry more food, split the gas money, have help when you need to change a flat tire, have someone keep guard for you when nature calls (don't forget the "mountain money"—toilet paper), have more people to throw rocks at that deranged-looking guy with a thirty-six-inch chainsaw who is walking through the woods looking for unsuspecting victims, etc.

Bowling

Before you go, create a different way to keep score.

The guy has to use the heaviest ball he can find.

You have to change bowling balls every three frames.

Every other frame you've got to close your eyes right before you throw it (no peeking).

Miniature Golf

- Guys have to putt with their opposite hand (unless the girl is on the golf team).
- No keeping score.
- Whoever gets the most strokes wins.

County Fairs

Don't play any of the dumb dime and quarter games that are guaranteed to rip you off. Stick to the 4-H exhibits.

Go Fishing

Test your patience and the potential for future fun by making sure the other catches fish first.

Roller Skating

There's just something about doing the Hokey Pokey with a hundred strangers, isn't there? Hey, if you can stand the music they play, you can laugh at each other, fall down a lot, do the limbo, hold hands, show off, get sweaty, drink soda, waste a buck or two in mindless video games, share a locker, watch *other* people fall down and get sweaty . . . the possibilities are endless.

Horseback Riding

Whether you're experienced or not, this is can be a blast. Do it on a Saturday so you have Sunday to recover.

Zoos & Aquariums

It's not just for kids anymore. You'll get a few laughs, learn something about God's creation, and be able to spend two to four hours together asking some of the questions in the back of the book!

WHEN BREAKING UP IS RIGHT TO DO

No dating relationship will last forever—unless you get married—and most teens know they'll actually date *several* people before they decide to make a lifetime commitment to *one*. But how do you know when to break up? When trying to decide whether or not to break up with someone, it's wise to talk things through with an adult, with someone who's been there. Still, here are a few clues to help you know when the time is right to call off the relationship.

Forced Feelings

If you have to *force* yourself to get psyched-up about going out with someone, it's time to call it quits. A good relationship is one you *enjoy*. If you're having to *make* yourself feel good about being with someone, it's not genuine. And it's only a matter of time until your lack of sensitivity really hurts the other person.

Spiritual Straying

If the guy or girl you're dating isn't drawing you closer to Christ, chances are he/she is drawing you further from the Father. You may be thinking, *OK, so Brad's not a Christian. That doesn't make me any less of a Christian just because I'm dating someone who's not.*

Consider this: NO ONE remains neutral. You're either growing *closer* to Christ, or you're straying *away* from Him. No one can stand still for an extended period of time.

And it could be that you're so much "in like" that you don't even notice you're not as spiritually sensitive as you used to be. That's a dangerous spot to be in. Ask an adult you're close to—and one you trust, like your parents or youth leader—if they've noticed any spiritual changes in your life since you started dating your recent guy/girl.

Bottom line: As Christians, our major goal in life is to be as close to God as possible. If the person you're dating isn't helping you meet that goal, it's time to break up.

Handlin' the Heat

Is the guy/girl you're dating pressuring you in any way? There are several kinds of pressure: sexual, emotional, physical, social, etc. If you're being pressured to "han-

dle the heat," guess what? *You don't HAVE to handle it!* You can break up! Don't let *anyone* expect you to juggle unnecessary tension.

You don't attend R-rated movies? Great! Then don't be pressured into going to one with the person you're dating. You don't attend parties where alcoholic drinks are being served? We don't, either!

Don't think for a second that you have to "handle the heat." Simply refuse to be a part of a relationship that expects more than you're willing to give. You're uncomfortable kissing? Or holding hands? Don't continue to see someone who wants more than you're willing to give.

Crowded Corners

Are you feeling trapped? Need some space? This is a common reason for breakup among teens. When one person feels stronger than the other, it's easy to crowd their space. *No one* likes to feel trapped. If the guy/girl you're dating is calling too much, sending too many notes, or hanging around more than you're comfortable with, you're probably better off dating several people or just being friends with lots of people of the opposite sex.

Everyone needs their own personal space. If yours is constantly being invaded more than you like, consider getting out of the relationship.

Preoccupied Patterns

Are you just sitting around waiting for him/her to call? Pretty much scheduling your day, your week, your *life* around this person? Can we say you're *preoccupied?* If so, you're placing far too much emphasis on one relationship. Get up and get going! This person isn't the only one in the world who cares about you. Determine to become a more well-rounded person. Learn to care—*really* care—about others. And yes, it might mean you have to get out of the relationship before this can happen.

Ouch! That Hurt!

If the person you're dating is constantly putting you down, criticizing you, or making you feel bad about yourself, it's time to get out. The goal of dating is to become better friends with people of the opposite sex; and if your dating partner gets his thrills from stomping on others, then you're in a dysfunctional relationship, and he or she isn't the one for you!

Here are a few other signs of an unhealthy relationship:

Extreme jealousy: When your date can't handle you looking at or speaking to anyone of the opposite sex, or he/she reacts in an unrealistic manner in anger, withdrawal, or accusations.

Physical abuse: When your date hurts you physically. This could be a slap, a squeeze that's too tight, scratching, biting, kicking, punching, or knocking you down.

Verbal abuse: When your date curses, screams, or says derogatory things about you.

Anything ELSE?

Besides the reasons listed above, here are a few more clues to help you realize when it's time to call it quits:

- When you overhear your date refer to you as his/her "ex."
- When your date says he'll pick you up at 7 P.M. and he shows up at 9 P.M. with lipstick on his mouth.
- When the things your date used to do to make you laugh now make you angry.
- When you begin making excuses for his/her wrong behavior.
- When you begin to feel used or taken advantage of.

‖‖‖‖‖‖‖‖‖‖‖‖‖‖‖‖‖‖‖‖‖‖‖‖‖‖‖‖‖

Jamie Knew It Was Time to Break Up with Bo When . . .

- He kept calling her Marla.
- He insisted she change her hair color.
- He sent her a note addressed to Kelli.
- He always took the opposite side of everything she said.
- He never showed up on time and didn't bother calling to explain that he'd be late.

Mitch Knew It Was Time to Break Up with Angie When . . .

- She kept "fixing" his hair.
- She always agreed with everything he said.
- She volunteered to do his laundry.
- She started becoming better friends with his parents than with him.
- She asked a million questions about his ex-girlfriends.

CELEBRITIES' MEMORABLE DATES

Andy Landis, Christian Singer

My sophomore year in high school I was head-over-heels crazy about Warren. He was a wrestler and in my French class. I can still remember how my heart would race when he'd even *look* in my direction! He was a year older than me, and all my friends teased me about him. (Eventually *his* friends began to tease me, too!)

Well, the Sadie Hawkins dance was coming up, and with a lot of help from my friends, I somehow got the nerve to ask him to go. My palms were sweating, my heart was in my throat; but the words finally came out.

He said yes—and before we knew it—the night had arrived. I stood by his side the entire evening, not knowing what to say or do. I was dying from embarrassment. We hardly talked the whole night. We were both shy. We didn't like to dance much, and all of our friends were giggling and watching us. I sort of bumped his hand a couple of times hoping he'd get the idea to try and hold *mine*, but he didn't; and I felt like crawling under a rock! I was shattered.

But almost at the end of the dance, he turned to me, smiled, and said he was having fun. I was suddenly in heaven! I blushed for the hundredth time and forgot that I had tripped three times already and had looked everywhere but at him.

When we said goodnight, though, he gave me a big hug! I was ecstatic. Sometimes the most awkward moments turn out the best.

Kevin Mills, Newsboys' Bass Player

The best date I've ever had actually occurred after I was married. During the first couple of years of our marriage, money was tight. But I took what remaining money we had and hired a limousine to pick us up at our house at 7 P.M.

We enjoyed two hours of cruising around town, dinner, and stopped at the riverfront. After our limo ride was over, we checked into the hotel I had reserved for the night.

Unfortunately, because a convention was being held at this hotel, there were a lot of people running up and down the halls, screaming. We decided to leave that hotel and check into another, but it was sold out. We tried another, but it had only one room with two single beds—not the ideal sleeping arrangement for a first anniversary.

We eventually ended up back home, thankful that together we had both experienced our best date ever.

Heather Floyd, Point of Grace

The best date *I* ever had was with my best friend's husband. Of course, they weren't married at the time and she was dating another guy, but the four of us all went out one evening.

We went to the State Fair, rode the rides, and went to a free country music concert. Afterward, we went two-steppin'. It was my first time to go, and we were twirling around and everything. It was so much fun!

Then we went to an old, old building that was empty. It had been vacated and was really dark. It had all sorts of boards and stuff everywhere, but we climbed up to the very top. It was one of the tallest buildings in the city. The moon was shining, and we just sat there and sang and talked for the longest time.

Ashley Cleveland, Recording Artist

The most memorable date I ever had was the night the man who's now my husband first kissed me. We were business acquaintances for seven years and gradually became friends and bandmates. Over the course of a year, our feelings grew into something deeper than just friendship.

We were both extremely cautious, however, feeling there was much at stake personally *and* professionally—and we held out until we couldn't deny it any longer. It was a kiss containing all the passion that had been building for a year! Seven months later, we got married.

Terry Jones, Point of Grace

The day I got engaged was the best date I ever had! Point of Grace was in New York City to perform for a benefit at Radio City Music Hall. While there, we went to the Plaza to have tea, then we walked to Central Park. As soon as we got down the steps in the park, he proposed. It was so beautiful! The sun was setting behind the buildings of the city, and I was almost numbed by it all.

I quickly said yes, though, and we went on to Radio city Music Hall for the Rockettes Christmas show. Afterward, we went to the Rainbow Room and to the city Christmas Tree and watched the skaters. It was incredibly romantic!

Shelley Phillips, Point of Grace

The best date I ever had was with my college boyfriend. He surprised me one afternoon while we were at school. We drove to the airport in Little Rock, then flew to Dallas, Texas.

He had a dress made especially for me—a real fancy one with gloves and everything. I had to change in the ladies room on the plane. When we got to Dallas, he had rented a fancy car, and we drove to dinner and then to the opening night of *Phantom of the Opera!* We caught the return flight that night and went back to school.

Jody Davis, Newsboys' Guitarist

Around Christmas one year, in Jackson, Mississippi, the city decorated the park downtown with the most breathtaking display of lights and decorations that I and my future wife had ever seen.

One cold night, Erika and I bundled up and strolled through the park, eating freshly roasted peanuts and listening to the Christmas music. The evening was topped off by a tremendous fireworks display which was so close to us, the flames didn't die out until they had streamed through all the trees around us.

We were married in a church across the street from the park one year later.

Denise Jones, Point of Grace

My favorite date was after we were married. When Stu and I were dating, we never got to spend a February 14th together because I was always on the road. Last Valentine's Day was the first time we ever got to spend this holiday together.

He really surprised me! He had told me what time to be ready and what to wear, but that was all I knew. Around 7 P.M. a limousine arrived. I'd never ridden in a limo before, and it was really exciting.

Stu gave me a rose and took me to a special restaurant for dinner. Afterward, we went up to the Pinnacle (a revolving restaurant on top of a hotel that overlooks the city) and had dessert, then drove around in the limo and went home. I'll never forget that night.

Andy Landis

The best date I ever had was on the night Steve Buckingham asked me to marry him. He told me we were going to a picnic and to wear comfortable clothes. He picked me up in a red Bronco truck, and we drove to the hills outside of Nashville. We turned onto a dirt road, then drove onto a tall, open hill.

The sun was just beginning to set, the air was crisp, and the wind was blowing.

We drove past running horses and grazing, curious cows, all the way to the top of the hill.

Steve told me to go play with the horses while he set things up. He put a blanket on the hood of the truck and lit some candles, then called me over to sit on the truck. Next, he handed me a music box. As I opened it, it played "Amazing Grace."

"Look inside," he said. I peered a little closer and pulled out a ring as Steve knelt down on one knee in front of the truck. "Will you marry me, please?" he said.

The sky was so blue—and so were his eyes! The air was so clean—as were his hopes for us. The night was so romantic, and I already knew he was the man God wanted me to spend the rest of my life with. I nodded my head and whispered, "Yes."

"What?" he said.

"Yes!" I answered. "Yes, YES, *YES!*"

Shelley Phillips, Point of Grace

It seems like we were on the road *forever* last summer! I had one night at home, and I was going to pack to go back out again. The guy I'm dating was in town, but I didn't think we'd have time to get together because of his schedule.

He didn't have a meeting after all, and we ended up going out to eat. We went to Granite Falls (it's a neat restaurant in Nashville), and we ate out on the patio. It was late so there was hardly anyone there. It was very quiet and beautiful outside. We had not had much time to spend together, so were really grateful we finally got some quality time. We sat out there talking until the restaurant closed!

Brian Barrett, Christian Singer

Since I have a private pilot license, I rented a place and took my date on an evening plane ride. This was in West Texas and the sunset was astonishing—especially at seven thousand feet! There were so many different shades of blue, yellow, and purple that it was hard to believe it could get any more beautiful . . . until the stars began to appear. Slowly, the night sky was *covered* with a blanket of shimmering lights.

I wasn't sure if my date was in awe or just air sick; she didn't say much. Maybe she just didn't trust my piloting skills. At any rate we had a great time, and it's certainly a treasured memory!

Andy Landis

The most creative date I ever had was really just a "friends date." We had burgers and fries at a drive-in place, and he stuck French fries in his mouth like an elephant and blew bubbles in his Coke. Then he slapped his burger and threat-

ened to throw it like a Frisbee. He was hysterical! I was laughing so hard I could hardly eat.

Well, we were already late for the movies, so we went to the store and bought really dumb, cheap presents with our movie money. You know—those sixty-nine-cent items at the check-out counter in the drug store?

Then we drove to a bunch of our friends' houses and put these little gifts on the porch with their names on them along with a note about friendship. We rang the doorbell and hid until someone came out. We ended up going to about a dozen houses. The more we did it, the better we felt. Everyone *loved* getting those ordinary little surprises! We never told anyone it was us—we just let them wonder. It was great!

STRANGERS ARE PRAYING FOR YOU

You haven't been prayed for by name from these strangers—but with God, of course, that doesn't matter. It perhaps hasn't been consistent, but that doesn't mean they're not serious about heartfelt pleadings to the God who promises to one day answer.

What are they praying about? Let's listen in to see if we can hear . . .

Lord, I pray for the young man who will one day marry my daughter. That he would be a man who loves You with his whole heart; that he would even love You more than he loves her. Protect his heart and mind, Lord, so that he would be

able to love her with a love that's pure. Remind him to pursue You above all else. Place around him Christians who will not just point him the way, but be the example he needs.

I don't know who this man is, Lord, but help him this day to respect the girls in his life. Help him not to be overcome by passion for another, but to keep himself sexually pure for their wedding night with our little girl. Bring him into her life at the right time. May their marriage be a light to all who see them together for many, many years. Amen.

If you're a Christian guy reading these words, it's likely your parents have prayed something similar about your future bride (why not ask them?). They know it will benefit not only you, but themselves for decades. You see, nothing rips the heart out of parents faster than to see a child they spent twenty-plus years investing their life in, choose a mate who isn't the answer to that prayer.

Your teenage years can be wonderful. We can testify that you'll measure most of your life by how many years it's been since you graduated. It's like the beginning of adulthood. Unfortunately, we've seen hundreds of men and women make life-altering mistakes during these beginning years that affect them for a long time. The number-one culprit that scars a life is how they treated—or were treated—by the opposite sex before they were married.

> ⊡ Did her boyfriend treat her like a unique creation of God, or did she allow herself to be used?

> ⊡ Did he hold in high regard that girl he spent time with—respecting her

WHILE YOU WAIT▼

above his own lusts—or was he more interested in having a story to tell friends?

Did the young man or woman realize they had been prayed for by strangers—dozens, perhaps hundreds of times?

If you've been given permission to date, have chosen to date, or are currently dating, have you thought about what it means to be 100 percent successful with the opposite sex? Do you want a dating life you won't have to regret? Then use these ideas, statements, and questions to help.

Be the one who is setting the pace by committing from this day forward to date differently from the rest. Allow the prayers of strangers to make a difference in how you treat the opposite sex. Remember, for most who read these pages, marriage will be a lifetime commitment. The best gift you can give your future mate is a pure mind, heart, and body on your wedding night. If this is your goal above all else, you'll know what it means to be 100 percent successful with the opposite sex.

"I've actually had many romantic and memorable dates with Amy, and the best ones were always sort of spontaneous and unplanned. Like the time last fall when Amy and I took my Harley for a spin down the Natchez Trace and all the leaves were turning. We stopped for a picnic along the way. I'll never forget that day, and neither will she."

Gary Chapman, Christian Singer

THINGS YOU NEED TO KNOW ABOUT GUY/GIRL RELATIONSHIPS

- The person you're dating is a unique creation of God. He made only one of each of you, and as much as He loves *you*, He loves the person you're with, too. Treat that person like he/she is one of a kind.

- The other person has a present he/she wants others to invest in, but he/she doesn't want to build a bank account of regret.

147

- Like you, his main priority needs to be his relationship with God. If anything—or anyone—takes His place, he's in jeopardy of being influenced by the evil one.

- Listening to someone is far more important than talking.

- Desiring someone's body does not mean you're in love with him/her.

- It's easy to make someone feel inadequate if you criticize or compete to win at everything you do.

- Learning to like someone is far more important than worrying about falling in love with him/her.

- Girls expect guys to read their minds. Unfortunately, guys try to do it. Learn to ask questions and say what you really think.

- Complimenting one's character is tougher, but probably more important, than complimenting appearance.

- Simply watching TV or movies together won't build your relationship—at all!

- If you're tempted sexually, God provides a way of escape well before the motor is running in third gear. Learn how to recognize where that escape is.

- Pointing out faults in another doesn't help unless you point to solutions.

- Using humor at the expense of someone you're with is definitely unacceptable.

- Just going for walks together may well be the best times you ever have.

- Never go into a relationship trying to change the other. You probably can't do it anyway, and it's a bad goal to shoot for.

- Relationships will teach you more about forgiveness than anything else.

- Ask your parents what "manipulative statements" are. If the one you're with uses them a lot, you're in *big* trouble.

- Guys: Respecting your date above all else will mean you will never lack female companionship.

- Memorize 1 Corinthians 13:4–7 before you ever start to date.

- Girls: Watch how your date treats little children. That will tell you more about his character than a hundred dinners and movies together.

- Phone calls to parents when you're going to be late aren't optional.

- Don't talk that much about your date to your friends while you're in the relationship, or after it is over . . . unless it's good stuff.

- Learning how to enjoy someone's company without spending a lot of money is a lifelong skill you'll want to learn.

- Small gifts on a consistent basis mean more than big gifts once a year.

- Every relationship will have problems. How you handle them is what counts.

- The person you're dating will blow it! That's OK. So will *you!* Be flexible and allow room for mistakes before you write the whole thing off.

- God loves the person you're dating as if he/she was the only one in all the world!

- *You* have the power to make the person you're with feel good or bad about himself/herself. Use this power wisely. Make time to affirm and encourage.

- Realize you don't *have* to have the last word on everything! The sooner you learn this, the better your relationships will be.

- A small surprise goes a long, long way. Surprise your date with something inexpensive but meaningful.

- Do you like the shirt he/she's wearing? Say so!

- It's someone who's secure in himself who'll take time to build up someone *else*.

- Many people think relationships are 50/50. Instead of striving to maintain a *balance*, try to *out-give* the one you're with!

- Keep thinking about the future and if this person will be a part of it or

WHILE YOU WAIT ▶

not? STOP! Enjoy the *present!* Let GOD handle the future.

- Going to church together will deepen your relationship.
- Girls, watch how your date treats his mom. This will give you MAJOR insight into how he views women!
- Spread some positive gossip about your date.
- No matter how irritated you may get at your date, *always* be kind.
- When in doubt, ask "What would *Jesus* do?"
- Always *thank* your date for your time spent together.
- Listen. Listen. Listen.
- Smile a lot. A little bit of cheer goes a long way!
- *Everyone* loves to be around someone who laughs. Learn to laugh—even at *yourself!*
- Girls, if you've been dating a guy for some time, offer to pick up the tab once in awhile.
- Guys, don't get in a rut. Just because you've taken her to dinner *before*, doesn't mean you have to do the same thing again. Be creative! Think and plan a fun, variety-filled evening.
- Girls, never take a date for granted. Of everyone he *could* have asked out, he chose *you!*

- Girls, when participating in a sport with your date, don't simply give up and *let* him win. Every guy enjoys a challenge!

- Guys, NEVER think that when a girl says "no" she really means "yes."

- Have you discussed last Sunday's message with your date? If not, what are you waiting for?

- Do you want to be a success with the opposite sex for a few years or your entire life? Always keep the big picture in mind.

- Guys, if you comment about a girl's hormonal time of the month, you're an insensitive lout. Get a life!

- Don't be a pest on the phone. If the conversation's going nowhere, call back another day when you have something to talk about.